# GRACE in DEEP WATERS

## VICKI L. KEMP

*Largo, MD*

© 2021 Vicki L. Kemp

All rights reserved under the international copyright law. No part of this book may be reproduced or transmitted in any form or by any means, electronic or mechanical, including photocopying, recording, or by any information storage and retrieval system, without the express, written permission of the publisher or the author. The exception is reviewers, who may quote brief passages in a review.

ISBN 9781562295165 Hardcover
ISBN 9781562295202 Paperback

Christian Living Books, Inc.
P.O. Box 7584
Largo, MD 20792
christianlivingbooks.com
*We bring your dreams to fruition.*

Unless otherwise indicated, all Scripture quotations are from the King James Version of the Bible. Scripture quotations marked NIV are taken from the Holy Bible, New International Version®, NIV®. Copyright © 1973, 1978, 1984, 2011 by Biblica, Inc.® Used by permission of Zondervan. All rights reserved worldwide. Scripture quotations marked NKJV are taken from The New King James Version / Thomas Nelson Publishers, Nashville: Thomas Nelson Publishers, Copyright © 1982. Used by permission. All rights reserved.

---

Library of Congress Cataloging-in-Publication Data

Identifiers: LCCN 2021026784 (print)
Subjects: LCSH: Consolation | Grace (Theology)
Classification: LCC BV4905.3 .K449 2021 (print) | DDC 242/.4--dc23

# ENDORSEMENTS

"It's amazing to know someone like Lady Kemp, who has a deep understanding of God's grace. *Grace in Deep Waters* is not a vague and airy-fairy collection of various points of view. Vicki unveils how grace will cover your eyes against what you're going through and make it easier to manage life because you don't feel the weight of your problems. This book is biblical, personal, and healing. It will have you clinging to the merit of Jesus Christ. I highly recommend it."

**Supervisor Barbara Bryant**
Best-Selling Author of *Favor, Blessing, Increase (FBI)*
Los Angeles, CA

"Grace is a sweet friend and a loyal presence" and so is Lady Vicki as she takes us on this journey to know grace. With every fiber of her being and every stroke of her author's pen, Lady Vicki longs for each reader to experience the multifaceted awards of grace. Grace affords us what we don't deserve while shielding us from our penalty paycheck. So, get acquainted with grace, accept grace, and allow the sweet friend of grace to cover you while the Master Physician, Himself, intimately and intricately administers treatment for every emotional hole in your soul leading you to that healed place … "All Because of His Grace."

**Pastors Roland and Marisa Banks**
Compassion Christian Center
Bakersfield, CA

"Everyone wants some grace applied to their lives, but it is important to know that the grace you receive is the grace you give. God's grace is huge; it reaches everyone. It's a gift that is freely given. We live, move, and have our very being because of the grace of God. This amazing book *Grace in Deep Waters* will walk you deeper on your grace journey by opening your hearts and minds to receive God's grace. Though we sometimes do not think we need, grace is with us always."

**Clinton and DeAnna Lewis**
Authors of *Faith Family and Franchise*
Franchise Owners of Wingstop and Fatburger Brands

"Lady Kemp is more than just an author; she is a dear friend whom I have known for nearly 30 years. She and my wife have been sisters for 40 years. She has lived a purpose-driven life dedicated to ministry and the transformation of people. *Grace in Deep Waters* is more than just a book. It is a vehicle to help transport people from their past to a brighter future. In this transformative literary work, she illustrates how God's unmerited favor upon our lives will strengthen and regenerate us. You will walk away understanding the gift that is God's grace, which is freely given to us all."

**Brandon Shelton**
National Division Director, Common Spirit Health
**Regina Shelton**
State Farm Claims Representative

"This book is a classic, comprehensible, and compassionate piece of writing on the virtues of grace. It is a relevant and required reading from the heart of a woman who has become an expression and example of God's grace. Our culture has become so contentious with condemnation and accusatory language that it was time for Lady Kemp to answer the call to speak words of consolation and comfort to the church and culture. You will find understanding, sensitivity and sensibility to whatever challenges you face in life. This book is raw, real, and relevant. Who would have ever thought we would be blessed with a sista-friend who exudes this thing called Grace? When you come to know what you know, you accept and embrace the burden of sharing what has been instilled in you. How can the mere subject of 'Grace' become a Master Class you ask? Read this book, written masterfully by Lady Kemp, then share AND adopt the principles. We are all made better because of the sufficiency of Grace."

**Bishop Broderick Huggins**
B.A. Huggins Ministries
Gospel Without Borders Seminary and Bible College
**Lady Toni Huggins**
TM Huggins Enterprise, LLC

"God's grace is a gentle friend that is kind, merciful, and forgiving when we don't know how to be that to ourselves. Grace is something we can never earn, but it is extended to us from God because He loves us. What people must understand is being in deep waters of hurt and painful memories is a journey. Healing will be a process and you will need God's grace every step of the way. God's grace is new every morning. He will give you grace every day to work through those deep wounds in your heart. You will learn how God's grace will carry you through every pain you decide to get healed from."

**La'Drea Luckey**
Master of Social Work (MSW)

"Grace is like a breath of fresh air; you know that it is there, but you can't see it. Grace is something that no man can truly and wholeheartedly give to another. Grace is God's unmerited favor stored up for the just and the unjust. When I hear the word "grace" it reminds me of my Lord and Savior Jesus Christ and how He died on the cross for my sins and the sins of others. The sufferings He endured allow us to have grace. God's grace is sufficient. In the chapter entitled, "Grace," Lady Kemp describes the trials and tribulations we go through in our lives. The way Lady Kemp associates grace with strength is priceless. She describes grace as strength that is bestowed upon one when he/she becomes broken. That is so true in more ways than one. Grace and strength go hand and hand. As I look back over my life to see how God's grace has saved me from danger seen and unseen, I lean back in my chair, shake my head, look up to the Lord, and say, "Lord, thank You for Your grace."

**Mechelle D. Henry**
Laborer for the Kingdom
MPA/BA Criminal Justice

# DEDICATION

To my husband and my best friend, I call you "Dear," for you are dear to my heart—my joy of 29 years. You help me to be better than yesterday. Your encouragement has been my strength and anchor. I love you for pushing me. The lessons I have learned from you are for a lifetime. I honor you as my bishop, my leader. You are a transformational leader and above all the titles, you are an incredible father and husband. Thank you, kingdom man, for being the husband God made just for me. I love you forever and forever is a long time. You are my secret keeper and a sweet melody I sing daily.

To the loves of my life, our amazing children: Bryan and Alexandria, my reminders of God's favor, ambitious dreamers, and creative giants on the earth; Alexis, my reminder of brilliance and creativity, my giving and loving baby girl; Javon and Arniesha, my reminders of talent, intelligence, and sweetness coupled together; Marvin, my reminder of a champion and protector of the family; Charrell, my reminder of gentleness, harmony, and love. I pray for you more than I pray for myself. I feel blessed to be your mom. God knitted us together as a remarkable family. Thank you, children, for being my teachers and cheerleaders. I declare that you will have an incredible future and because of grace, you are triumphant in all you set your mind to do. I pray I will always be your strength, help, and example. I love you more than the words in all the books ever written.

To all my grandchildren, our gifts from God, whom I love so dearly—you bring the family so much joy. Each of you has a unique style and personality. I am ecstatic for the newest gift to our family, Brentley Dakari Guyton—what a joy given from God, born on September 29, 2020.

Thank you to my parents, Papa and Coco, the late Daniel Webster and Cora Mae Jordan, for instilling in me the importance of loving God when I was a child. I am forever grateful for my heritage and pureness for God because of you. Your resilience has taught me how to conquer and soar. I am favored to be your daughter. I have witnessed your sacrifices and love on many levels. They are unmatched. Mom, you are with me at 91 years of age. That is grace. I continue to learn from you. You are an incredible, godly woman of great wisdom. I am in awe of your zeal and strength. Thank you over and over for teaching me how to be a woman and how to show love in spite of. I love you.

# CONTENTS

*Introduction*   xi
*The Prayer of Grace for Today and Beyond*   xv

Chapter One – **Grace**   1

Chapter Two – **Let's Go Deeper**   11

Chapter Three – **Grace in Weakness**   17

Chapter Four – **The Flood Has Receded**   25

Chapter Five – **Grace to Shift**   31

Chapter Six – **Swimming Lessons**   39

Chapter Seven – **The Broken Pieces Saved My Life**   45

Chapter Eight – **My Little Sister**   51

Chapter Nine – **Grace Period**   59

Chapter Ten – **Grace for Today**   65

Chapter Eleven – **Between Dilemma and Deliverance**   71

Chapter Twelve – **God's Glory**   81

Chapter Thirteen – **Still Waters**   89

Chapter Fourteen – **Relentless**   101

Chapter Fifteen – **Grace Wins**   111

Chapter Sixteen – **Sea Sickness**   119

Chapter Seventeen – **Deep Waters**   123

*Life Lessons*   128
*Other Books by Lady Kemp*   154
*Acknowledgments*   155
*Special Thanks*   157
*About the Author*   160
*Endnotes*   162

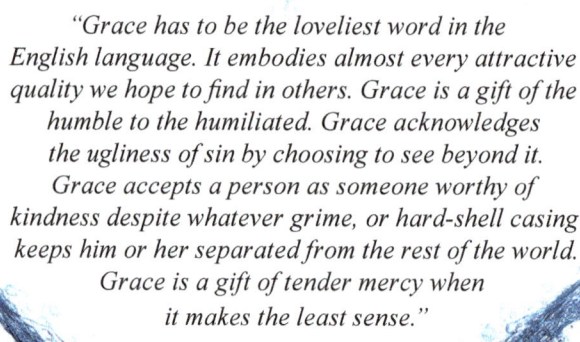

*"Grace has to be the loveliest word in the English language. It embodies almost every attractive quality we hope to find in others. Grace is a gift of the humble to the humiliated. Grace acknowledges the ugliness of sin by choosing to see beyond it. Grace accepts a person as someone worthy of kindness despite whatever grime, or hard-shell casing keeps him or her separated from the rest of the world. Grace is a gift of tender mercy when it makes the least sense."*

**Charles R. Swindoll**[i]

# INTRODUCTION

### I Pray You Learn How to Swim

Bitterness, negativity, insecurities, anger, and unresolved issues can become your prison leaving you in a false reality that is crafted by the Enemy himself. As a result, many fail to realize the power of God's grace. In fact, many do not even know what God's grace is. We hear several words exchanged about but seldom do we take the time to define them. "Grace" is one such word. What does it really mean?

Grace is the strength bestowed on us when we are bleeding, broken, confused, torn, and done with trying to figure out the part of life that makes no sense. Let us all admit we have experienced dark, bleak, and difficult life experiences that don't make sense. You feel as if you are in a sea, an ocean with clusters of seaweed and rubbish, mangled in the rocks and repeatedly hit by the high tides of muddy water. Life itself has a way of provoking you to quit trying to be the person you always dreamed of becoming. Or it can discourage you from trying to live a life of peace and harmony. However, grace is the friend that gives you the strength to rise and move forward. Admittedly, moving forward can be scary. Why? We fear any fall or disappointment ahead may be worse than the last time. Moving past the very thing that caused you to be stuck in the first place can be intimidating. It takes lots of energy to swim to the shore.

I heard someone say they have been through so much that anger and bitterness make them feel strong. They take all their painful emotions and transform them into an engine that keeps them moving. Is this thought process one you should adopt? No. It is a lie. Deception! See, the Enemy grooms us by planting little destructive suggestions in our minds. He does this with the intention of driving us into a deeper sense of confusion, which will ultimately cause us to lose everything. Do not let the wrong narratives fuel your mind. Do not allow your life to be powered by negative energy. You must take all the cycles of negativity and channel them to a place of healthy growth. It is vitally important to find the right channels that let you take a deep, honest look within and dig out all the junk, which is dormant, masked, hidden, and sealed by pain and insecurity. Unseal it; take the lid off, and expose everything in your life that keeps you buried in the depths of shame. A friend once told me, "Shame will make you walk around with an invisible billboard attached to you. You feel it and you assume that others see it and know your story." Shame is a tool the Enemy uses to keep us from seeing our purpose.

Like the ocean, there are many things in our lives no one would ever be able to dig out. It's too deep. It's too difficult. It's too heavy. It's not possible. But grace covers and maneuvers through all the difficult, heavy garbage in our lives making it possible for us to live in accordance with God's Word. Your truth enables you to live. But lies cripple you! They hide the truth and stop you from living in it. Don't you dare allow your false reality to limit you to the Enemy's boundaries and bind you with his handcuffs!

When we deal with ourselves, it is suggested we look in the mirror. The mirror means much more than just seeing a reflection. It is your reality. Surreal. When you fail to take a deep look in the mirror to disclose the flaws and disappointments, you betray yourself. Listen, facing your truth can be terrifying–but take courage. If you are ever going to be free from your past, you must start by being vulnerable with yourself. You are strong through the eyes of faith. That's it!

*Grace in Deep Waters* is me bearing witness to how our great God has been present in my life at each point. His grace has been constant. The deep waters represent lessons in our lives of the bad, ugly, hurtful, and challenging experiences we have all had. Like me, I am sure you have been in deep waters and God rescued you from drowning. Grace is that sustaining presence.

In this book, you will find gentle reminders of grace. I highlight stories from the Word of God when grace was present. You will also read constant reminders of how the Enemy operates for he is relentless! I use similes and metaphors to encourage you to examine your life and see how grace has been at work in you. I am not an expert, but a writer inspired by the Holy Spirit. This is a book of thoughts and truths that will inspire you to see the beauty in life, but you must do the work to enjoy it. We are not perfect. We live in a real-world with real problems. We all have a "from," a point where our journeys began, but with God's grace, we are going somewhere. The truth is we do not have to live in deep waters. We have a choice. I pray by faith that this book teaches you how to swim.

**Because of His Grace**
**Vicki L. Kemp**

## *The Prayer of Grace for Today and Beyond*

Heavenly Father, we thank You for this space of grace that has been afforded to us. It is grace that abounds even in the midst of unwarranted, unprecedented environments. Your grace surrounds us, covers us, provides for us, protects us, and exudes light in a dark and cold world. Your grace abounds.

Thank You for this grace that superimposes itself over fear. It cancels out fear. It trumps fear. 2 Timothy 1:7 declares that You did not give us the spirit of fear but of power, love, and soundness in our minds. Lord, we thank You for this immeasurable grace that runs deeper than the ocean, higher than the heavens, broader than this planet we call the world. Your eternal never-ending grace will never cease to be. It will not suffer or experience diminution. Grace is the sum of Who You are. That grace!

Lord, we thank You for this unmerited favor that surpasses humanity's understanding. Thank You for Your saving grace, the gift of grace, something we can't earn or take credit for. It is freely given because we believe in You. For it is by grace we are saved through faith and not of ourselves; it is a gift from You, O God (Ephesians 2:8).

We are so grateful for this amazing grace that has been set as a foundation, a platform that provides standing strength in deep waters.

Ephesians 1:19 declares that Your grace is efficacious through the exceeding greatness of your power. In this dispensation of grace, Lord, I thank You that I can approach Your throne of grace with confidence to receive mercy and to find grace and favor to help me in my time of need (Hebrews 4:16).

Lord, I thank You that through You, I have access by faith into this grace in which I stand and rejoice in the hope of the glory of God (Romans 5:2).

Lord, I thank You that sin is no longer my master because I am no longer under the law but under grace (Romans 6:14).

Grace for today and beyond, in the matchless, magnificent, majestic name of Jesus Christ, we pray. Amen.

**Bishop Vernon R. Kemp**
Greater Harvest Christian Center
Bakersfield, CA

## Chapter 1

# Grace

Lights. Camera. Action. Have you ever felt as if your life was on the big screen? All eyes were on you. You and everything about you were highlighted for the world to see. Picture this! The film is rolling; yet, you don't know how your story will end. God has the script. He is the author. He has written the story of your life. He has all the rights reserved and no infringement on copyrights are allowed. There is so much in the detail. Plans, expectations, dreams, hiccups, lessons, and seconds chances–things you haven't read yet.

God has each step and every season of your life already planned. Nothing you do will catch Him by surprise. Even when you make the worse mistakes and stumble on disappointments, don't forget God has already seen all of it. God has already been where you are trying to go. God is infinite, and He has a timeless existence. From everlasting to everlasting, He is God (Psalm 90:2, ESV).

You ask yourself the question, "How in the world is *this* going to turn out?" It looks impossible. It feels impossible. The voices in your head state, "It is impossible." Life appears to be too much. Weighty. Grim. Unknowing. The grey areas in life are always the ones that keep us thinking. The thought of it all is heavy on your heart and mind. It is hard to breathe. It is like holding your breath underwater, running short of air, and fighting to get to the top to rejuvenate. It is tough. The pressure rushes to your heart and the burning sensation in your lungs makes you feel as if your head is about to burst. To exhale is life. Let's try it.

> *Quick! Take a breath and try to hold it. If you reach 11 minutes and 35 seconds, congratulations! You are now tied for the world record. For most of us, the ability to hold our breath lasts 30 seconds, maybe even 1 or 2 minutes. Much longer than that and the sensation that your lungs are bursting becomes too painful to endure. Breathing of course is a reflex action; we do it more than 19,000 times a day automatically and without thinking. And while we can intentionally control the pace, rhythm and depth of our breath, the overall voluntary ability to override our own respiration is very limited.*[ii]

Limited, yes. Why? God is the One Who controls every ounce of our beings. He is the One Who allows us to breathe. He holds our breath. Life is in His hands.

Life has a special way of teaching you when to fight to live, even when situations and statistics deem you done. Completely done! At times, we will question the path we are traveling on. We will question the unknown areas in our lives as the circumstances, experiences, and relationships are unclear. There will be times when we cannot see what God is doing. There will be moments when we must trust God's plan for our lives, even when we may not know where we are going. We must learn to trust Him despite the uncomfortable places and unsure circumstances. You know those places. They are dark with heavy terrain and are difficult to maneuver. We are travelers, so we know the ropes. However, at those times, the roads we travel are rough, paved with stones, pebbles, debris, stickers, and detours. It is only by God's grace that we stand in confidence to make it through.

## No One Is Exempt

Without God's amazing grace, where would we be? Take a moment and reflect. You had a wow moment, huh? We would be somewhere trying to exhale. That question is cliché, but it is a reality check for all

CHAPTER ONE - GRACE

of us. Do you hear me? All of us. No one is exempt. I have pondered this many times before, sometimes several times a day. Sometimes I have that type of day that makes me remember. It is by God's grace I rise. I breathe. I function. Despite me. It is by God's grace I have not drowned in my thoughts and afflictions.

Our thoughts get in the way. Can you relate? Despite my perception of how my life is supposed to be, according to *me,* God has sustained me. I know without a doubt there are specific times in my life when God's grace covered me. I am still here–physically, emotionally, and mentally. It is by God's grace that I can think. Yes, think! I can touch and feel. I can hear. Grace has carried me. And ditto for you too. Grace is a sweet friend and a loyal presence. Do you feel favored knowing grace is that sweet friend? We can sleep at night with this assurance.

As I reflect, there were times when I focused only on my flaws. The Enemy has a cunning way of setting you up to fail. He causes you to rehearse the negative narrative, rather than embrace the positive, the beautiful, and the effort. I was *totally* in an emotional place. Women, we know about emotions, don't we? And men, yes, you also know. Emotions can take us to a place of no return if we allow them to. Here is the deep part–I hid my flaws very well (exhale). Well, at least, I *thought* I did. Now and then, my flaws would shine through resulting in an emotional meltdown. Yes! Tear, panic attacks, and spiraling back and forth in thought, all that. However, grace covered me in my secret place during those times. My secret place is where I release my insecurities (lack of confidence and doubt). Those insecurities were me not feeling good enough and second-guessing who I was called to be.

## The Cry of Victory

Have you ever had those days you wanted to lay in bed in a fetal position? It's okay to have a moment, but you must get up and tackle the day. If you don't deal with insecurities, they will follow you for the rest of your life. You can develop into a reckless mess. If you don't deal with stuff, yes stuff, or talk about it, nothing will go away. It will just get deeper. The plot will thicken and layers continue to form. It will stay and stick to the part of you that is weak and eventually, an explosion will take place sooner or later causing harm to you and others. Insecurities also keep you as a victim. They cause you to prey on others to complete you and cater to those insecurities that call for change. Anxiety is birthed from insecurities that will keep you going in circles and cycles. What is the one insecurity you are dealing with right now? _____ .

There is grace for it. I write this crying. But it is a cry of victory.

> He that dwelleth in the secret place of the Most High shall abide under the shadow of the Almighty. I will say of the LORD, He is my refuge and my fortress: my God; in him will I trust. (Psalm 91:1-2)

## CHAPTER ONE - GRACE

*It is by God's grace
I rise. I breathe.
I function.
Despite me.*

In the secret place I go. I run there. I pray fervently. Why my secret place? It is comforting. I can function most of the time but in the secret place, I am vulnerable. I can cry and not worry about my tears being judged. You pause right here. Think about your tears. Many times, we are judged by our tears. I am sure you can relate. In deep waters, although broken, I found comfort in knowing God would put me back together piece by piece. In that place, I could be the real me. Raw. Honest. Uncut! (deep exhale). The most freeing feeling in the world is being able to bare your soul to God. No fake smiles. No makeup. No playing "the happy" or "I'm blessed today" roles. In this place, there is no pretending. Freedom! Liberty! I did not need to pretend at all. I did not have to smile or give hugs to those who caused me anxiety. I did not have to make excuses for their rudeness–and I might add–mean-spiritedness. We encounter people who are just nasty. But God sees it all. And I admit, He sees us too (laugh out loud). Oh, and He hears everything. Listen, life has taught me that sometimes it is not people; *it is us*! As you see others, see yourself and evolve. Besides, don't allow people to interrupt what God is doing in you.

I was most curious in my secret place although I knew the Word of God. When you are striving to get to that special place in God, distractions come–unnecessary thoughts. I needed to focus on myself. Do you get that part? When you are trying your best to get to a place in God, the Enemy brings distractions to take your thoughts to insignificant places. However, God would often snap me right back into shape by reminding me to worry about me. God always has a way of chastising me gently. "Vicki, you are in My presence. All the extra stuff is not important!" Thank You, Lord, for the gentle reminders.

## Inhale and Exhale

This journey in life has taught me many lessons, and I'm sure it has taught you also. You need to get it together. It is you. The first step in getting yourself together is loving you. Value yourself. While in the secret place, close out the world; inhale and exhale, and release all the stuff that causes you to panic keeping your mind in shambles. Sometimes we are in our way. We get in our own way by playing God. We give God our problems but when He does not act fast enough, we pick the problems right back up. Friends, God does not need our help. He is God. He is the almighty God. Period.

I prayed my most authentic prayers before God in my secret place. I dealt with the ugly stuff the average person would be ashamed of. I mean, I prayed messy prayers–my truth. I could be myself without reservation. I remember being so frustrated within my spirit because I wanted things done my way, but God faithfully whispered, "Relax; trust Me to work out the part you cannot see." Remember, He has written the script. God's got me. He has you too. Aren't you grateful? Gratefulness is being so close to God that His Spirit often prompts us to trust His character rather than our very own. He gracefully broke me down by reminding me if I was going to be in a secret place with Him, I needed to concentrate on Him rather than the weight of yesterday or the stress of the current day. God constantly crossed insignificant things off my list and rearranged my mental priorities. He knows what we don't need to give our attention to. He canceled all distractions, and I always settled in peace.

*In the secret place truth shows up and freedom touches heaven.*

The beauty of being in the secret place is that truth shows up and freedom touches heaven. Our Father in heaven releases the grace to triumph. If I was upset and did not feel like talking to anyone, I did not have to. Have you ever needed just a minute? I was able to wrestle within myself and release my frustrations to God alone without feeling obligated to explain anything to anyone else. Sometimes we must give ourselves the time and permission to deal with matters of the heart–quiet time. Quiet time is not feeling pressured to answer the phone or return text messages. Does this sound familiar? Can you relate? On your knees, prostrate before God–that grace moment is priceless.

If you are truly honest with yourself, you will recognize the parallel of my secret place experience with your own. We all have them, and I'm sure we have all been there. The secret place matures into a healed place. A transfer takes place. The healed place makes a difference in your life as restoration takes on a whole new meaning. I knew I was messed up in my mind due to my perception of what others thought about me. The secret place allows you to deal with all of this, every part of your being. Now, I get it. Who cares? Stop it! Why do so many of us care so much that caring becomes a huge distraction in our lives, which causes us to be bothered in our thoughts. It took a minute to get it but I got it.

## Just Live

If I could ever encourage others, I would tell them to live. Why? You were created to live, not merely exist. Unfortunately, many people remain statistics because they allow the opinions and sentiments of others to kill their ambitions. You must get to a place in life where you are unbothered. Free! Of course, freedom is a process for many. It was for me. God, thank You for the grace to be delivered from people. Thank you, Jesus.

I was also held hostage by my mess-ups. I could not release it all in my first book, *Better than Yesterday*[iii], but by grace, I will continue to share the truth to set others completely free. I have made many decisions in my life that I'm not proud of. What were those decisions? Well, I know one decision was loving hard when it was uncomfortable and unhealthy. Another decision was not letting go when I should have.

I knew what to do, but I let the Enemy keep me stuck. I was trapped in my mind. I dare say we've all been here.

I learned we allow people to occupy spaces in our lives where they do not belong. Those negative spaces cause us to rehash the poor decisions in our past that bind us in shame and denial. Some decisions I've made were tied up in my emotions–wild and free–running all over the place. They literally put me through mental anxiety. Not good. I know. Thank God, I was able to speak to myself in that not-so-good place while in the secret place and remind myself that I would not stay stuck. I declared it! I pursued freedom. Even in my anxiety, my mother's prayers and God's Word did not depart from me. The Enemy had a plan, but the beauty is God did too. I could not see it, but He was working things out on my behalf. He is the Author of our lives.

> And we know that in all things God works for the good of those who love him, who have been called according to his purpose. (Romans 8:28, NIV)

It is all working out. All the mess that concerns us is working for our good. God was at work on my behalf during the bleak times in my life. I can testify He has the best bailout plan. Even as I wrote this chapter, I found myself reflecting on those experiences and feeling even more grateful for God's grace than I ever did before. Friend, there were times when I would mount the pulpit to speak while bombarded by grim thoughts. Though it appeared I was present, in my mind I was distant, pondering the thoughts of yesterday, mistakes, misconceptions, perceptions, questions–stuff–insignificant stuff, but stuff that was consuming my mind and consuming it well. While reading this chapter, you are probably saying, "Wow!"

Well, what is your story? You might know what I am talking about. The Enemy's plan was for me to fail but my faith was in God. I refused to let the Enemy take my faith; it was not up for grabs. Grace! The Enemy's goal was to embarrass me before my peers. His ultimate plan was to make me the laughingstock of the church. Has this ever happened to you? Have you ever been consumed by a dark cave of thoughts? Have you ever longed to be free? Perhaps you were not in a place to stand before others and deliver a message. Maybe you had to give a presentation at work or school, but your mind was not in the right place. Nevertheless, grace covered you as it covered me. Aren't you thankful for grace, which shines from heaven enabling you to move forward? Grace is that superpower which picks you up when life has given you a good, old-fashioned beating. Grace is that presence which shields and comforts you when the Enemy wants to make you relent, run, and wallow. Grace is a friend that says, "Get up! I got you." Grace says, "Shut up the voices in your mind. I am here to make it all better." If you can identify with grace, shout aloud, "Thank You, Lord!" I can hear you shouting. I can feel it too. Take a moment. Rejoice!

> *Grace is a friend that says, "Get up! I got you."*

## *Oceans (Where Feet May Fail)*

You call me out upon the waters
The great unknown where feet may fail
And there I find You in the mystery
In oceans deep
My faith will stand

And I will call upon Your name
And keep my eyes above the waves
When oceans rise
My soul will rest in Your embrace
For I am Yours and You are mine

Your grace abounds in deepest waters
Your sovereign hand
Will be my guide
Where feet may fail, and fear surrounds me
You've never failed, and You won't start now

So I will call upon Your name
And keep my eyes above the waves
When oceans rise
My soul will rest in Your embrace
For I am Yours and You are mine
And You are mine

Spirit lead me where my trust is without borders
Let me walk upon the waters
Wherever You would call me
Take me deeper than my feet could ever wander
And my faith will be made stronger
In the presence of my Savior

Oh, Jesus, you're my God!

I will call upon Your name
Keep my eyes above the waves
My soul will rest in Your embrace
I am Yours, and You are mine[iii]

## Chapter 2

# Let's Go Deeper

What is grace? Grace is enhancement, honor, adornment, and protection. Grace is the favor of God. It is the enabler that pushes us with power. Grace is a necessary gift from God for growth and improvement. Without God's grace, we cannot overcome certain confines and weaknesses. Grace is the stimulus that catapults us forward, onward, and upward. Grace is the Spirit of God functioning on our behalf to renew and strengthen us. Grace is supernatural help from God; it is that gentle reminder that taps you on your shoulder amid a fiery trial and says, "Hi, I'm here." It is the quiet voice that visits us at night when we are tormented with unrest and whispers, "It's okay; go to sleep." Grace is the calm that takes the sting away and whispers, "Yes, I am with you in the fire. Obey, and I promise to bring you out." Now and then, God will send us kind reminders of those who made great sacrifices; nonetheless, grace carried them.

> And of his fullness have all we received, and grace for grace. (John 1:16)

There are many compelling stories in the Word of God. One of my favorites is the story of Mary and Joseph. It is a story that's familiar to many, and its message is true and clear. Mary was an empty vessel–pure, indeed. It was evident that God took delight in her. God filled her with His grace, and she was fruitful for His glory. She was specially chosen to carry out His promise to redeem the world. She was handpicked by God to be the mother of Jesus. Yet, many called her flawed due to the nature of her story. It was considered ugly by the gossipers. Many took pleasure in reveling in gossip then as they do today.

Even with our flaws, we can show the world God is great, and He allows things to manifest to demonstrate His ability to shine in deep, dark situations. God has a fascinating personality. I learned that our flaws and mishaps–as embarrassing as they may be–are worth it. They all have a purpose although the process of finding it does not feel good. Mary's story was so worth it. She had the unique honor of bringing Jesus into the world for us–not just for me or you, but for us. Let us look at the miraculous event in the lives of Mary and Joseph:

> And in the sixth month the angel Gabriel was sent from God unto a city of Galilee, named Nazareth, to a virgin espoused to a man whose name was Joseph, of the house of David; and the virgin's name was Mary. And the angel came in unto her, and said, Hail, thou that art highly, the LORD is with thee: blessed art thou among women. And when she saw him, she was troubled at his saying, and cast in her mind what manner of salutation this should be. And the angel said unto her, Fear not, Mary: for thou hast found favour with God. And, behold, thou shalt conceive in thy womb and bring forth a son, and shalt call his name JESUS. (Luke 1:26-31)

Mary was known as a peasant girl, but she was a vessel of grace. When reading the birth story of Jesus, it's easy to overlook the pain of Mary's experience because the outcome is so beautiful–extremely beautiful! Think about it. The ridicule and shame Mary must have experienced were heartbreaking. Tear-jerking. I am sure it was very painful. She may have even questioned her purpose. Have you? Many times, she may have asked herself, "Why?" She may have even directed that question to God Himself. Her life was indeed a movie that would be played before the world without her permission.

CHAPTER TWO - LET'S GO DEEPER

Some deemed the movie–her movie, her life–a lie. God had invaded her private space, turned her world upside down, and selected her to be a chosen vessel. What was her conversation with the Lord? I wonder what she thought of her life. How could a virgin explain this situation in a way that people would believe her? Our societies have shaped us into valuing the opinions of others so much, we feel we must justify everything to them, even our responsibilities to Christ. But no, we do not!

"I'm pregnant, but a man has not touched me." This makes no sense. What do you mean you are pregnant, but you didn't have sex? It cannot happen this way. It's impossible! I can only imagine their taunts, the whispers, lies, and gossip she had to endure. If you have suffered any hardships, falsehoods, regrets, or mistakes, you also know what it is like to feel alone or isolated. Thank God for grace.

*Grace was there and where grace is, God is present.*

Thank God for Mary's strength. Mary submitted her life to God's will. Thank God for His choice in Mary. Do you get that part? His choice. Were you selected for something special, which you were not ready for? I have always found it interesting that Scripture never mentions Mary's lineage. Where was her mother or father during this time? Can you imagine being in this situation without a family to support you? Who was there for Mary? Mary did not have any physical support system beyond Joseph. However, grace was there. And where grace is, God is present.

When others do not understand the instructions God has given us, how do we react? How do we respond? How do we continue moving forward when it just does not make sense? It is because of grace we don't go crazy–literally–crazy! When we experience great challenges, God's grace keeps us from breaking, bending, and crumbling.

- ♥ Grace is God giving us a supreme treasure we don't deserve
- ♥ Grace will help you handle situations when under pressure
- ♥ Grace will bridle your tongue
- ♥ Grace will cause you to be gentle
- ♥ Grace will cause you to walk in love
- ♥ Grace will help you hold your fists.
- ♥ Grace is greater than we can imagine
- ♥ Grace is the power to help someone through their conflicts

## Capacity to Hold

Grace undergirded Mary with the strength to grow. In my spirit, I hear one word: capacity! Mary was favored with grace and capacity. Mary was a vessel of grace used by God. Hence, she went through what she did without failure. When the angel spoke to her and said she would have a Son, she never pleaded her case or asked why. She held her peace. She would hold and carry the gift God had given her. Mary received God's word because she was pure. She submitted to God despite the perils. She was ready. Her heart was right. Her spirit was open to receive. So it is with us. Our capacity depends on what we can hold. Can God trust us? Despite our flaws and thinking, we must choose to be great in tough, seemingly unsurmountable situations.

Grace helped Mary carry Jesus. The angel of the Lord reassured Joseph of the gift to Mary. See, at times, we don't understand the acts of God. We don't get all the facts: we just don't. We may not even know the why behind it all, but we must trust God. It's okay. Grace shines in the darkness of the unknown. It meets us there.

Grace is something we don't deserve. It is a gift we are given regardless

## CHAPTER TWO – LET'S GO DEEPER

of our worthiness to receive it. It is the unmerited favor of God, a gift that only God can give. Mary had no idea she was even being considered. She had not completed an application or expressed interest in the job. But God had plans for her life. Big ones! God had her purpose wrapped up in His plan (deep sigh here). His plan. What an honor from God! That is how favor operates. Grace helped Mary accept the call. That same grace does the very thing for us.

Before I married and became a pastor's wife, I remember saying to the Lord, "Really? Me, God? Why me?" To be honest, I did not want to be a pastor's wife. Nope! I felt too much was packed in this role for me. Many times, I convinced myself I could not do it because there were too many grey areas. My life would be one of great sacrifice. My life would be as living in a fishbowl. All eyes on me. I just did *not* want to be a pastor's wife. I was afraid, had my own theories, and admittedly, I was downright insecure.

God extends grace when we do not want to do a specific task or carry out our gifts and callings. But capacity was also extended to me. God freely gave me the time, as well as the emotional and physical stamina to do the very thing He wanted me to do. At times, I think I was a bit different from Mary. I voiced my feelings, whereas she kept quiet. I cared too much about what others thought, but Mary could not care less. Now, as I reflect, I realize God gave me the capacity to serve when I did not think I could. Grateful! Do you hear me? Completely grateful! I had no desire. None. I'm just being honest. Just like Mary, God's grace helped me carry out the call on my life. God is doing the same for you, too. God gave me the strength, wisdom, and ability to deal with the call and the love to believe in it. I am now excited about my journey and I adore serving. We see the love of God through His grace, and we see it clearly.

Let's go deeper.

Think back on a time in your life when you went to the wrong place; you had no business being there. Grace covered you in moments when you spoke the wrong words and the time you acted totally out of your character, Grace shielded you. Aren't you glad? God's grace doesn't ask for credentials or a resume to cover you. Grace doesn't require you to fit into a certain group or class. You do not need the experience man asks of you. Grace does not judge or seek approval. Grace is an amazing gift. It is simply given.

Mary was picked and favored for kingdom purposes. She was set up for greatness. When you have the grace of God, His favor, you can have what God says you can, even though people say you are not qualified to get it. It is His grace, not the people's grace. You can be what God says you can be, even when others say you will never amount to anything. Grace allows us to do what we cannot do for ourselves. It equips us to stand and positions us for victory. It causes the vessel–me, you, us–to do great exploits for God's glory. Grace puts us in execution mode, readies us to act, deliver, and move forward in the things of God. Grace makes things–the right things–happen. Take a minute right now and thank God for His powerful, undying, remarkable grace! "The will of God will never take you where the Grace of God will not protect you." –Author Unknown

## Chapter 3

# Grace in Weakness

Grace runs as deep as the deepest sea. Like the sea, grace is continuous; it travels for miles without end. If you ever gaze upon the ocean, you will see the water goes far beyond what our eyes can behold. It transcends what we can imagine. The beauty of the sea takes you to a deeper understanding of the creative power of God. It is simply amazing. The power of God helps us to understand that when we are weak and tired, God's grace runs as the water: deep. It is incomprehensible. Grace covers you.

I recall a time hearing a powerful lesson on grace by Javon Kemp whom we call Pastor J:

> *When you have a great call and a great assignment in your life, great challenges will come along on your journey. The greater the challenge the greater the grace. The greater the assignment, the greater the grace. Grace is a gift that provides favor which is an act of kindness beyond what is due or usual. Grace is something you cannot earn. The grace that man functions in has nothing to do with what you have done. Grace is like an usher that is happy to meet and greet you at the door and show you to your seat in God's presence. God has draped us in grace. Grace makes what we do look easy but if they only knew the back story.*

It's the back story for me. Apostle Paul also reminds us of the sweet power of grace that covers us just as the sea travels for miles and covers the earth. Grace is our declaration that in our times of difficulty, it is the nucleus that holds us together. It is the core, the center, the heart.

Grace is our great God displaying His love to us when we don't deserve it. There were so many times in my life I didn't deserve God's grace. You can't earn God's grace. Grace is strength when we are in the deep, dark places of life. It is freely given to us. Aren't you thankful for grace? I am thankful beyond words. In our weak moments, we would do well to remember the Word of God which declares:

> My grace is sufficient for you, for My strength is made perfect in weakness. Most gladly, therefore, will I rather glory in my infirmities, that the power of Christ may rest upon me. Therefore, I take pleasure in infirmities, in reproaches, in necessities, in persecutions, in distresses for Christ's sake: For when I am weak, then am I strong. (2 Corinthians 12:9-10)

That is such a powerful scripture for the believer to meditate on. In our times of affliction and weakness, grace shelters us. It is the healing balm for our afflictions, illnesses, and diseases. Many believe affliction is a punishment from God. They place this explanation of afflictions on others as if God agrees. Don't allow people to capitalize on your experiences making you feel as if the test you are going through is because of sin in your life. Do not measure a person's walk with God by their circumstance. Could it be that our God desires we learn from these experiences, so we are confident we will overcome the next problem? Grace reminds us that affliction is not always chastisement from God. Sometimes it is from a different source; nevertheless, it visits all of us. We live in the real world and we are human.

As we just read, Paul humbly boasted in his affliction. He knew he was strong in Christ although he was feeling weak. His strength was perfected in weakness. How is this even possible? God had a proven track record with Paul. He was confident in the power of God, which he knew by experience is great. Paul was resilient because of Christ, which caused him to have a champion mindset. I'm sure he spoke to his mind through faith. What I love about Paul is he was not afraid to acknowledge or too proud to confess that he was weak. He wasn't ashamed of his affliction. He was so solidly assured in Christ he could confidently say he was strong. Paul knew the Enemy would never get the glory based on what he was enduring because His destiny was in the hands of God.

## Sufficient Grace

The Lord declared to Paul His grace was enough. As a result of this sufficient grace, even in Paul's weakness, the Lord could be shown strong. When we stand in the strength of the Lord and not in our own, our Lord's power is perfect. Complete. And when we lean on the Lord or look to Him in our hardships and brokenness, we are made strong. Should the Lord choose not to remove the area of weakness, He can use it for His glory!

*You must pursue peace in your affliction by working God's Word.*

God was Paul's strength in his weakness. Once Paul understood this, he could rejoice, even in his frailty. As a believer of Jesus Christ, there is no need to be ashamed of weaknesses or frailties. It's called humility. I now know that I can openly speak of the areas in my life that seem weak or broken. At one point, rejection broke me, but grace mended me. I am a rejection specialist. However, because of His grace, I too am made strong. I can now demonstrate to you how to be healed and win. I can passionately teach you how to speak your truth and move on in life. God's grace is sufficient. God wants to use those weak areas and frailties in me to show His strength. His grace is truly enough! Therefore, we can do *all* things through Christ who strengthens us (Philippians 4:13).

The experience we endure now will bless others later. My friend, can you also boast in your afflictions knowing God, our God, has an antidote? Have you, too, been tried although you have a peaceful perception... because of grace? You must pursue peace in your affliction by working God's Word. Working the Word is reading and living the Word. I realize when I open my eyes in the morning I have a choice to be positive, no matter what I am facing. Being positive is standing firm in the faith. God persistently restrains the heavy pressure we should actually feel in our afflictions. I'm sure you can attest that at times when you dealt with pain, death, sickness, disease, or calamity, our good God eased the pressure. Grace in weakness!

In retrospect, I recognize the Enemy will even make things appear as if it is in real-time. Lies... the Enemy presents so many technicalities.

By God's grace, we realize that while in affliction, God's strong righteous right hand is with us. He is with us! Trust this assurance. Sadly, at times, we cannot govern what we suffer; however, we can govern our responses to our sufferings. We must respond the righteous way and recognize that grace carries us when we cannot carry ourselves. When we are fragile, we are strong in the grace of God. We will experience affliction, but we must manage our afflictions God's way. Allow afflictions and weaknesses to be the vehicles that drive you where God desires you to be in Him. God wants to bring abundance and wisdom to us. The reality is sometimes they only come through our afflictions. David gives insightful information about the tough reality of afflictions.

> It is good for me that I have been afflicted, that I may learn Your statutes. (Psalm 119:71, NKJV)

David proclaims it was good for him to be afflicted. How? He gained so much from it. He was enriched and strengthened. Isn't it amazing that some of us come to know God at a deeper level when we endure affliction? You are afflicted, but your understanding of God's grace, love, and compassion are indeed evident. When you spend time with God while going through, wisdom shines and lessons are birthed from experience. Thank you, Lord, for the lessons that have been birthed from afflictions. We learn our God is sovereign. He is a healer and mind comforter. God is the bridge that gets us over to the other side. God is the source of joy while in discomfort.

## A Big Test

While writing this chapter, the Holy Spirit reminded me of a time I was afflicted with an ailment. It was August 2017, and I was prepping to teach at a women's retreat in Milpitas, CA. While driving on the freeway, I began to feel the tension and a throbbing in my head. The pain was excruciating. The agony and tension in my eyes were terrible. As we made it to the hotel, we checked in and headed to our rooms; unfortunately, the pain in my head grew worse. Worrying thoughts and uncertainty ran through my mind. "What is going on, Lord? I have to speak in the morning." I rebuked fear in Jesus' name. This experience was a test for me. A big test! I was determined not to fail the people but primarily, I did not want to fail God.

Determined to finish the assignment, prayer was paramount. Constant prayers of healing and thanksgiving were my focus at this point. Naturally, I also took Motrin as I thought it would help to ease the pain; however, there was no relief. I applied hot towels to my head–no relief. I was in no condition to concentrate or study the lesson I would teach the next morning, but I attempted to do so anyway. I closed my Bible and my eyes. The pain and discomfort were awful. Nevertheless, I knew, by faith, when I awoke in the morning, I would feel better, and the pain in my eyes would be gone. The next morning came. What I believed and felt I needed so badly was not the case. There was no relief. Yet, I was determined to push through depending on God totally and despite how I felt. When you stand in faith, although the answers to your prayers have not yet manifested, continue to believe. Faith moves forward faith has no reverse.

I declared healing in my body in Jesus' name. Although weak and pained, standing in the strength of God was my stance. My strength was made perfect in weakness. God showed Himself strong as I taught the Word of God. People were blessed, and they never knew how much pain I was experiencing. Listen, although afflicted, I denied my flesh and refused to give in to how I felt. I honored God and said, "Lord, you be my strength, and I will give you all the glory." God did that for me. Through that experience, without a doubt, I know God is faithful. Grace carried me forward to a new feeling of gratitude. We know God at a deeper level when we go through His way. I don't just believe God is a healer. I *know* God is a healer.

> He was wounded for our transgressions; He was bruised for our iniquities; the chastisement for our peace was upon Him, and by His stripes we are healed.
> (Isaiah 53:5)

His stripes were for the healing of a nation and they were also for me. The Devil has won some battles, but he will not win the war. Every one of us can sit at the feet of Jesus, learn about His nature, and have a deeper understanding that causes us to see His glory. It is clear. God, we see Your hand while going through. We must take the test and pass. We must study the lessons and learn. I see God working behind the scenes more often now. Before, I recognized it less. I understand now that while going through, we must trust, even when we cannot trace.

Thank God for His grace in weakness.

When we have exhausted ourselves, and we can't depend on our understanding and capabilities, grace is there. When the Enemy comes in like a flood and trouble is on every side, grace is there. Listen, when we want to give up and throw in the towel completely, we can rely on God's divine strength. How many times have you wanted to throw in the towel?

I have discovered God doesn't promise an easy life. He said in this world, we will have persecution, pain, trouble, and adversity; we will experience affliction. However, grace causes us to function with power and anointing.

## You Have What You Say

We are favored with a secret element: grace. As God pours into us, we pour out to others that they may be encouraged and strengthened. We invite others to experience God's grace that flows upon and through us. When you are weak, declare you are strong. Open your mouth and affirm it on the earth. Be reminded of this:

> Death and life are in the power of the tongue: and they that love it shall eat the fruit thereof. (Proverbs 18:21)

You have what you say. What are you saying about your situations, afflictions? Are you speaking life?

Paul was admired and praised because he was truthful and gave vital evidence about the power of God. If Paul was ever going to be strong, it was when he had moments of weakness. His mind was strong. His declaration to himself was strong. He was determined and resilient. Paul reminds me of a champion. The grace afforded to Paul deemed him a champion in every way.

As Paul said, when I am weak, then I am strong. Paul spoke life. Paul had hope in the Lord. The strength of God is released when you are weak. God does not aid us to do what we can achieve for ourselves. He supports us when our power does not exist. When we are weak, God is mighty to save us. Thank you, Lord, for grace in weakness. The strength Paul talks about is the strength of a champion. Grace is the gift that helps the champion fight when there is no more fight in him. When you have done everything to stand without falling, the champion allows you to keep standing. Grace is manifested in our lives and allows us to stand beyond our natural strength. The only way we can come through the vicissitudes of life is with the power of God resting inside us.

We are still fighting this good fight of faith and the comfort is in knowing we have Jesus on our side. So while we are fighting, we must take on the posture of a champion. Because Jesus Christ is the ultimate, undefeated heavyweight champion of the world, we are champions. Because Jesus is, we are. The Word declares in 1 John 4:4, "Greater is He that is in us than he that is in the world." Champions stand secure when others around them fall. Although trouble and afflictions are coming from every angle and the Enemy is intensifying his attack, the champion in you intensifies. Inevitably, we will have suffering moments. The reality is we will take one blow after another, but the joy of the Lord is our strength.

The apostle Paul reminds us to take pleasure in infirmities, in criticism, in necessities, in persecutions, in distresses (mental suffering, hardships, and physical pain) for Christ's sake. For when I am weak then am I strong. The sea runs deep, but grace runs deeper. It sinks in all the afflicted places of our lives to rejuvenate and renew.

Grace declares: "You are still here. You are still fighting. You are a champion!"

## Chapter 4

# The Flood Has Receded

Elevation! Foothills! High places! Tough terrain! Unfamiliar territories! Mountains! Have you ever been in a position where you could not see the top of the mountain in your life? Your view was cloudy and gloomy. The overcast thoughts blurred your perspective on life making it confusing because *so* much was surrounding you. In life, there are hills, peaks, and highlands you must climb over. Despite our backgrounds, nationalities, ages, education levels, or economic statuses, we will all have to ascend a tough mountain or two in our lifetimes. Mountains can be intimidating, overwhelming, and steep–especially if you have to actually climb them. There is consolation, though. Our great God assures us He will help us as we climb and walk with us through stormy weather. Just as God remembered Noah, He will also remember us.

> And God remembered Noah, and every living thing, and all the cattle that was with him in the ark: and God made a wind to pass over the earth, and the waters assuaged; The fountains also of the deep and the windows of heaven were stopped, and the rain from heaven was restrained; And the waters returned from off the earth continually: and after the end of the hundred and fifty days the waters were abated. And the ark rested in the seventh month, on the seventeenth day of the month, upon the mountains of Ararat. And the waters decreased continually until the tenth month:

in the tenth month, on the first day of the month, were the tops of the mountains seen. (Genesis 8:1-5)

- ♥ The waters ceased
- ♥ The waters abated
- ♥ The waters were restrained
- ♥ The waters decreased
- ♥ The waters stopped

This was an act of God's grace. Noah himself found grace in the eyes of the Lord. God told Noah when the flood would come. However, Noah had no idea when it would cease. Sometimes this is the case with us. We question how long we will go through life's storms. How long will they last? Life is filled with uncertainty. And we must admit the Enemy creeps up now and then to give us a good fight. Satan is thorough. He is ruthless and obsessive about his plans to defeat us in life's storms. But he also knows if we hold on to God, God will see us through completely.

The flood Noah experienced was an inundation of the land. You may ask, "Where was the levee?" Levees are intended to guard against flooding; however, they can and do decline over time. They can ultimately fail over time. Just as life experiences and circumstances arise, so do floods. They can occur without any visible sign of rain. Did you catch that? Floods can occur without any visible signs.

Life just happens.

## Prepare for Flooding

Noah was prepared for the flood. Likewise, it is important for us to prepare for flooding no matter where we live or who we are. We are human, and it is not uncommon to question the path we travel. Like me, I am sure many days you've wondered, "God, how long? How long must I tread water? How long will I have to deal with this?"

## CHAPTER FOUR – THE FLOOD HAS RECEDED

Reflecting takes me back to 2017 when I was writing *Better than Yesterday.* Hurricane Harvey had a part in the book's delay. Halfway through the editing process, Hurricane Harvey flooded the state of Texas. One of my editors, Sheila, resided in the small city of Baytown, Texas. The rain fell continuously. We waited for the rising waters to cease and recede. But the water increased.

Many people lost their homes, and businesses were destroyed. People within the city lost everything and life for them halted. Life was fragile and questionable, and feelings of emptiness hovered over the city. It was a complete nightmare. I will never forget Sheila calling me and saying, "My family and I are at our neighbor's two-story home. There are thirteen of us on the second floor."

Her family was allowed to remain in that home with the hope that Hurricane Harvey would stop. I can't imagine residing at a neighbor's home while looking down from their second-story window watching my home, belongings, trucks, and cars, flooding, and drifting down the street. The pain of loss. The pain of the unknown. People died in that horrendous flood.

Sheila shared with me the frightful experience as she and her family were rescued by boat. At the time, her daughter was pregnant. By grace, her grandbaby, a beautiful baby boy, Mylo, was born, and he is doing well. Grace covered and saved them. They were favored to have shelter, food, and comfort from those who loved them from near and far. Grace has a way of showing up when life threatens to fail you. Thank you, Lord, for the bountiful grace and mercy You have shown.

### The God Channel

Have you ever been in a situation when nobody could help you but God? The answer was Jesus. I, too, faced many situations in the past, and I had to get a hold of the loins of my mind. I was flooded with thoughts, possibilities, and what-ifs. I had to change from the *flood channel,* tune into the *God channel,* and begin to speak the Word of God in faith. During the flood, grace will equip you to continue to smile, laugh, serve, and work every day, even when you are shaking on the inside. Some days, you may find yourself crying in your sleep and trying to get in touch with God. Grace will carry you. The God I serve will be with you in the dirtiest places, and His love is a freely given gift. Receive the gift.

We have heard this declaration for years: "That which does not kill you, will make you stronger; that which does not crush your spirit will bless you." I have discovered that when you are in the midst of a flood or a storm that does not flee, God wants your attention. The greatest blessings can be found in turbulent times. There is something to learn. Most of the time, God is trying to teach us it is not about us; it never has been. It's about bringing Him glory. It is about making the name of the Lord great.

*That which does not crush your spirit will bless you.*

In our happy times, we tend to forget to show gratitude to God. I have also discovered that issues are allowed in our lives to make us think and mature. We encounter mountains and floods to bring us back to our first love: Jesus. How quickly many forget Who Jesus has been to them. We also forget that how we go *through* is important to how we come *out*. We bring glory to God by the way we handle the flood, how we maneuver through it, and how we treat others through it. The way we process the floods and storms in our lives is vital. We must endure and go through God's way. There is a specific lesson God wants us to learn for the next level, and we absolutely cannot defeat new-level devils with old mindsets. You cannot conquer the new with an old mentality. Just as we need a natural levee to hold when it floods, we also need a spiritual levee to prevent our lives from being flooded with life's deep waters.

## CHAPTER FOUR – THE FLOOD HAS RECEDED

Our spiritual levee is the Holy Ghost. He is our defense mechanism holding us together during the flood. He is our rest. He is our peace helping us not to break. I encourage you today to take advantage of your levee. Take advantage of the Holy Ghost.

> But you will receive power when the Holy Spirit comes on you, and you will be my witnesses in Jerusalem, and in all Judea and Samaria, and to the ends of the earth. (Acts 1:8)

The Holy Ghost is your protection during the floods of life and your strength to climb the mountains and tough terrains.

Noah depended on God, and God remembered Noah.

> And God remembered Noah, and every living thing, and all the cattle that was with him in the ark: and God made a wind to pass over the earth, and the waters assuaged. (Genesis 8:1)

God will not forget you. You must declare peace over your life and demand the storm to leave. I know at times the storms we endure are bad. Even so, declare all is well anyway. It is well with your house. It is well with your children. It is well with your finances. It is well with your health. It is well with everything that concerns you. I prophesy that by the time you finish reading this chapter, the heavy burdens in your life will start to fall off. Our great God will perfect all that concerns you.

In Genesis 8:5, we learn the waters decreased continually until the tenth month. In the tenth month, on the first day of the month, the tops of the mountains were seen. I do not know what month you are in, but you will see over your mountain. The Word declares the water decreased continually. Trust God that the flood in your life will decrease continually. Just as God spared Noah and all that was attached to him, so will it be with you.

## Chapter 5

# Grace to Shift

Was there ever a time when you were afraid to be who God created you to be? If so, why do you think that is? We push others to the top while settling for the back seat due to fear and concern we will not be accepted. Fear prevents us from moving forward and keeps us at a standstill. We are completely paralyzed. In our minds, it is easier to push others, rather than ourselves. We fear the spotlight forgetting God has already illuminated our lives.

Friends, I say this most humbly: God always shined on me. To me, this was a way of Him saying, "Daughter, when are you going to shine in your light without standing in the shade of others?" In other words, God was saying, "It is time for you to make a shift, a change." It was time for a special edition makeover. I needed a shift to move from the mundane, mental thinking to a mindset that creates motion and movement.

We are destined to be great, but we need to fuel our faith and get rid of cowardliness to be great. We must fuel our minds with God's Word– the very Word that was deposited in my heart when I was a young girl. I am most appreciative for my secret weapon: the weapon of faith. Grace and faith cover us. Faith is our assurance that our heavenly Father will not leave us stranded or abandon us when we feel less than enough. When we become exhausted from trying, grace and faith will work hand-in-hand helping us to keep going.

## Move! Shift!

You must learn to speak over your life. The words we speak fuel our shift to greatness. Life is in your mouth. Progression and greatness are in your mouth. Your future transitions to progress are in your mouth. Do not get comfortable and play it safe. Move! Shift! If you were ever like me, you were comfortable being comfortable. However, being comfortable will get you nowhere if you are indeed trying to get somewhere.

I don't know what God is calling you to do, but I know He is calling you to do something. As you embark on a new chapter, speak to the very thing in your life that has you stuck. Your voice is as deep waters traveling for miles destined to give aid, inspiration, or healing to someone in need. Your voice runs deep in the earth creating fountains for others to drink from. Scripture reminds us that our words will not run dry; they run deep in wisdom. Our words are our wellspring, our fountain.

> The words of a man's mouth are as deep waters, and the wellspring of wisdom as a flowing brook. (Proverbs 18:4)

The words I spoke over my life created the boldness and confidence I needed. They ran deep within the dry places of my life, cleaning and refreshing that *hidden* confidence, parts of which I had never experienced. Like pure water, it takes confidence to shine. I had confidence. I just needed to let it shine through. It was hiding, waiting to peek through the part of me that was not ready to totally walk in the light.

Answer this question. Do you tend to dumb down and shrink in size, fearful of what others think rather than just stepping out for *you*? We spend more time working to please others than we do ourselves. This inevitably causes us to take the long route to success. We stunt our growth by staying stuck for reasons we cannot explain. If you, like me, are ever going to walk in fierceness, the time to walk and shine is right now. The time to soar is now. If you are *ever* going to step out, now is the time to step out of your comfort zone and be the person you are in your dreams. You have the confidence. You have favor. See it. Speak it! Don't be blindsided by the noise–just keep moving in faith!

## It's Time to Shift

Life has a way of teaching you to win when others want you to lose. I encourage you to keep moving and soaring above all who say you can't. You can! You know you can win because you have already survived the wilderness experiences. God sustained you through it all. Didn't He? Take a minute and ask yourself that question. All you went through prepared you for who you are now. Now that you are trained in the areas where you were once weak, get up and be great. It's time to shift. The hand of God is on your life. When God has shown you something or placed greatness in your life, interference from near and far is inevitable. But keep going! Shift.

I always knew in my heart of hearts that I was called to do and be something great on the earth. Greatness was spoken over my life when I was a young girl. I knew I was special because I was different. Some things I wanted to do I just could not do. That inner voice constantly reminded me "You can't do that." I surely wanted to. That conviction in my gut would not let me act contrary to God's Word. Well, I had a few slip-ups.

My father was a pastor and my mother an evangelist. I sat under my father's leadership for 18 years. I will never forget the New Vision Church of God in Christ on Cottonwood Road. It sat nestled right in the heart of my hometown, Bakersfield, California. My father would preach as if he were preaching to thousands of people but most Sundays, there were just 60 of us maybe. My dear mother would sing and play the piano as if there was no tomorrow. The passion my parents had for ministry was unique. Their walk with the Lord was righteous and real. I remember Sunday school, Bible Study, YPWW (Young People Willing Workers), and the 6:00 PM night service. New Vision was where I learned discipline and obedience to God. As I reflect, I say it was worth it all. The church was worth it. I learned then that I was the church.

New Vision is where it all began. New Vision is the place that shaped me into my future self. It was the place where I learned to work hard no matter who was looking. I learned to serve God when the membership numbers were few. At times, only my mother, father, and brothers sat in the pews as my dad preached in the pulpit at church. See, it doesn't matter about the crowd. It doesn't matter who is looking. What matters is the heart that pushes to be great even when no one is looking. And I would add, the heart that shifts when others are talking negatively–nonetheless, you keep shifting.

I remember the times as a young girl my parents would make me sing solo after solo. In my mind, I would say, "Oh, Lord, people don't want to hear me." But my heart was ready to sing. I can say that with joy. In my heart, I was ready. See, at times, we are ready to be great in our hearts, but we do not know how to move forward with our lips and limbs. Do you get that? We don't know how to execute. There are just so many questions. What do I say to move forward? How do I act? Will they accept me? Will my gifts and talents be good enough? Get ready for it. It's already good enough. I said to myself, "Vicki, God has graced you to sing this same old song a thousand times." It is good enough because I am good enough. New Vision was my practice run, giving God my all. I learned to give God my best.

I came to know God when life was simple and fair. People loved for real and didn't get caught up in the drama. Grace covered me. The pure love was just so sweet and fulfilling to my soul. I served God when cooking and selling chicken dinners and making popcorn balls just to pay the church mortgage was fun. My mother and father worked hard. My father worked in the grocery store business and did odd jobs while pastoring until he grew ill. My mother worked in the hospital and kept odd jobs on the side. They did it all. Grace was their constant. Grace continuously gave them the courage to shift to new opportunities that sustained our family.

My brothers laugh and say I had it better than they did. Life evolves to be better over time. We never missed a meal or suffered due to lack. Grace sustained us. Grace was our family's faithful friend. If we were almost out of food, the need was always provided. Can you relate? This is where my character was shaped and my love for serving others developed while young in ministry.

In my youth, I learned working hard was the factor for success. In my youth, I learned my life would only be a reflection of what I worked hard for. In my youth, I learned grace would be continuous if I did not take advantage of grace itself. I learned early not to use grace as an excuse to mess up because there are consequences for playing with God. I knew better, although at times, just like the youth today, I needed reminders. And I got them.

## Effortless Greatness

Friends, my honest desire is to please the Lord in all I do. At many times in my life, a true fight ensued just trying to figure out how I would make greatness happen. My mom told me something valuable, "Daughter, make God's name great." Quickly, I learned to work hard, be consistent, persevere, and watch greatness show up naturally, effortlessly. You can't force greatness. Period. Should you try, your journey becomes strained and heavy. Think about putting a puzzle together. You can't force a piece to fit and squeeze in a place it's not supposed to be in. Where you are and what you are doing is where you are supposed to be. God is the genius Who shifts the pieces. God is the One Who ordains us and sets us apart for His glory. That is what my mom meant, His glory. I get it now. Who we are called to be forms in the womb. God knows our end from the beginning. As God spoke clearly to Jeremiah, He speaks to us.

> Before I formed you in the womb, I knew you before you were born, I set you apart; I appointed you as a prophet to the nations. (Jeremiah 1:5, NIV)

God is all-knowing. He is time, and He also exists outside of time. God had an awesome plan for Jeremiah even before he was conceived. Likewise, He has plans for you. He has plans that you will do great exploits on the earth. He has plans for you to win and not fail. It is an awesome feeling to know that before I was formed in my mother's womb, our great God had plans for my life. He had me on His mind. He has us, you and me, in His heart.

Grace got me here. When you feel as if you can't do the very thing in your heart you dream of, you can. Yes, you can! Believe in yourself. Period. Shift now. It's time to level up in your faith. Grace has you.

Grace is favor. It helps you do what you think you can't. New Vision Church is where my passion for ministry was seeded and began to grow. I would never have imagined in a million years that I would marry a man who would later be a pastor. I am now my mother. In retrospect, my husband is as my father was: a pastor (and now a bishop). He is his father; his father was a pastor. Grace was that constant *then*, and grace is our constant *now*. God formed and fashioned me to be fierce and genuine before my mother and father ever named me. How outrageous is that? That is amazing love. God set me apart. I knew I was different. God appointed me. I was selected and chosen.

## Finishing Grace

Understand, you are called to the nations. You have work to do, and you must get started. No time for excuses. No time for second-guessing and no time for retreating. Don't you dare go backward. Stand up! Step out! Be bold! You are equipped to make the necessary shift. You are equipped with a finishing grace to finish. In the words of Pastor Joel Osteen:

> *Live forward in faith. God is breathing in your direction with finishing grace. You must tap into it. Don't sit around in self-pity. You have the grace to finish. Don't talk defeat, talk victory. Quit telling yourself you won't make it. God gave you the grace to start, and He's giving you the grace to finish. Even in simple things.*[iv]

## CHAPTER FIVE - GRACE TO SHIFT

New Vision Church is where I learned the simple things. It is in the simple things we learn discipline to complete each task we set out to do. Don't let this world, situations, or people cause you to yield or question the very thing in your heart that God ordained you to do. Be fierce–the kind of fierceness that challenges the Enemy to stop–motionless, the fierceness that is activated with a kingdom mindset, rather than operating in the carnal.

Keep going in Jesus' name. Discouragement may come, but remember, it is designed to force you to become motionless. It will cause you to stay neutral. It's like driving a car. If you don't shift the gears, there is no progress. You are given options. You can shift from discouragement by rejecting it because it simply has no place in your life. When you reject discouragement, you reject its fruits:

- ♥ Fear
- ♥ Doubt
- ♥ Unbelief
- ♥ Defeat
- ♥ Failure
- ♥ Complaining
- ♥ Regret
- ♥ Misperception
- ♥ Lies
- ♥ Erroneous thinking

When you reject its fruits, you learn to leave behind the people that keep you bound. Sometimes they're loved ones. Sometimes they're good friends. Sometimes they're just attachments. I know you want to take them with you, but you can't. Actually, you can, but how will your journey be? Deciding to shift can be uncomfortable but essential for progress. And some people will fall off. I know you love them, but they simply can't go with you to the next level. This passage of Scripture spoke volumes to me:

> Now the LORD had said unto Abram, Get thee out of thy country, and from thy kindred, and from thy father's house, unto a land that I will shew thee: And I will make of thee a great nation, and I will bless thee, and make the name great; and thou shalt be a blessing. (Genesis 12:1-2)

We must heed God's Word. Disobedience has consequences. God told Abram to leave his kindred (family) and get out of the country. However, Abram did the opposite. Abram took Lot with him, which caused God to remain silent in his life until Lot left. If you are like me, you love really hard and you want to take some people with you, even when God says they cannot go this time. Love them still, but you must leave them. Obey the voice of God. Obedience is better that sacrifice. You must keep going. I must interject something my sister DeAnna told me that made me think deeper, "We want people to stay but people don't mind leaving you." The process of releasing people is difficult but necessary. Do not get confused with releasing and loving. You release those who are stagnant in your life so you can grow. Your growth demonstrates that the same God Who used you is waiting for them to make a shift so they can be used by Him also. The love never goes away. Remember the law of love.

> Let no debt remain outstanding, except the continuing debt to love one another, for whoever loves others has fulfilled the law. (Romans 13:8, NIV)

Someone owes love. Pay your debt. Be accountable to the word. God is waiting for you to go the distance to be a blessing to others. He has already given you what you need. You are equipped with insight, tools, and wisdom to share and shine on those who want to experience the change only Jesus can provide. Keep going; be confident, and know God has duly prepared you for a time like this. Remember those things you went through that got you where you are today? Yep, those things prepared you. You got this, sis. You got this, brother.

CHAPTER 6

# SWIMMING LESSONS

At the beautiful age of 52, I still do not know how to swim. Why not…after witnessing my mom take her daycare children and grandchildren to weekly swim lessons over the years? Why can't I swim? It seems quite odd when I think about it. I love water. The beachside is incredibly relaxing and refreshing to me. Though now, as I reflect, I always remained in shallow waters when in the swimming pool. I laugh just thinking about it.

I always attempted to swim underwater but seemed unable to learn to swim on top of the water. Maybe I didn't believe in the art of swimming–or was I afraid to learn? I felt as if the weight of the water was stronger than I was. Sometimes that's how life is: weighty. The water felt heavy, and it seemed intimidating; this was my perception. The depth of the pool made me feel as if the water would swallow and consume me. I did not think learning to swim was important because I avoided the water dungeon–the deep side of the pool–at all costs. When we are young, sometimes there are simple things we don't think are important. However, somewhere down the road, that simple task shows up in our lives and we learn it is absolutely important. It is necessary for living. It is beneficial to my life and who I am. Sometimes, you gotta learn to swim, even when afraid.

Attempting backstrokes or diving off the side of the pool was not an option for me. The one time I did try, I did a complete belly flop (in the shallow end). I never tried again. I laugh at myself because I am incredibly bold when I tell people I can't swim–as if I am proud of it.

Everyone's response is always, "Wait, what? You can't swim?" Nope! I can't swim. Don't get me wrong; I flirted with the water. Sitting at the edge of the pool and dangling my feet in the water was just enough for me to stay cool and know I was safe. I was quite comfortable in the shallow end. I was comfortable knowing I was in control, as long as I sat right on the edge of the pool. Think about it. Sometimes in life, we think we have total control–until God shows us otherwise. Our lives are in His hands. How awesome it is that we can run to Him and be safe when faced with life's trials.

I love to watch my family swim, dive, and float in our family pool. My daughters can hold their breath underwater for relatively long periods. It is a game to them, but when I watch them hold their breath underwater, I can't help but think about life. In life, each breath we take is a gift. At times, you will need to hold your breath. We learn to face stress and difficult life circumstances with grace while holding our breath in faith that all we face shall be well in Jesus' name. Keep speaking in faith. It is well. Grace gets you through the deep breaths when life attempts to take your breath away.

## The Struggle is Real

This reminds me of a family gathering my husband and I hosted at our home. Our backyard was filled with family members and friends. The music was loud, the food amazing, the children were playing with one another, and the swimming pool was full. Of course, they were adults present to keep a good eye on the children. But suddenly, my nephew, Darrion, fell into the pool. The frightening thing was he could not swim at all. I could not save him. My body froze, but my mind started running. "I should have learned how to swim." My daughter, Alexandria, tried her best to help him, but she struggled herself and was going underwater with him. The strength of the struggle was pulling her under the water. The struggle to not drown was so real, they were both losing the fight.

Let me caution you to be incredibly careful trying to help someone already in a struggle. You may lose in the process, especially if you don't have the tools you need to help. In this situation, my sister-in-law had the tools. Suddenly and surprisingly, my sister-in-law, Helen, Darrion's grandmother, quickly jumped into the pool and saved him. She jumped in immediately and broke up the struggle. This reminds me of how our faithful God jumps right in when we need Him most.

The Lesson…

Life has a way of sucking you under quickly, and sometimes others sink with you without notice and reason. Getting out of the water seemed impossible for my nephew Darrion. I could not help him. I can't swim. Serious regret! Thank God for divine protection. Helen had no fear; she jumped right into that pool with her clothes on (I'm chuckling now, but it wasn't funny then). She had the skill and ability. Her gut instinct kicked her right into shero mode. Here is the kicker–he fell into the shallow end of the pool. Even so, the shallow waters were enough to take him under. Why?

*Don't panic. Refuse to let the weight of fear cause you to sink.*

He panicked…

The fear of water caused Darrion to panic. The overwhelming feeling of water filling his mouth caused him to panic. The taste of chlorine caused him to panic. The feeling of helplessness caused him to panic. Also, others looking on, some just like me and unable to help, were panicking. I was panicking and screaming, "Lord, have mercy!" Helen did not panic; she was so focused on saving him, she had no time to even think about panicking. She knew how to swim. Fear did not grip her; doubt did not defeat her; neither did the yelling of those looking on distract her.

Don't panic. Stay focused. Refuse to let the weight of fear cause you to sink. Shift in faith and realize grace is the favor of God that holds us up when life wants to beat and defeat us. Grace is the lifeguard that will not let you drown. Grace is the virtue that enables you to swim when you want to drown. Remember grace is your superpower. Breathe! Don't panic! Keep swimming.

## Just Keep Kicking

Keep kicking even when your legs are tired and in pain. With each kick, you are building muscles to withstand future challenges as the deepwater weighs heavily on your lower extremities. You are getting stronger. Just keep kicking. Keep kicking, even when you feel the weight of life taking you under. Don't stop. Just as a swimmer doing backstrokes can't see the finish line but feels it in his gut, so you will need to rely on God's power, even when He doesn't feel near. You will win the race. You will finish. Be reminded with this confident word.

> I can do all this through Him who gives me strength.
> (Philippians 4:13, NIV)

You can do all things. Yes, you can by faith. Believe it. Speak it. Declare it. Decree it. See it. Believe in yourself. Be careful. Watch the Enemy. Backstroke when the Enemy presents anything contrary to God's Word. Listen, you must know when to retreat. Be alert and know when to resist the devices of the Enemy. Know when it is time to say, "No." Know when to say, "Stop, Devil! You are defeated." You must know when the Enemy has set you up to fail and not prosper.

> Submit yourselves, then, to God. Resist the devil, and he will flee from you. (James 4:7, NIV)

God has given you the strength to fly and soar. One of the most competitive swimmers of all time is Michael Phelps. He has won 28 Olympic medals. He is indeed an Olympian. He is noted for his powerful race in the butterfly stroke. I always took pleasure watching Michael Phelps in the Olympic Games as he would plunge up and down in the deep waters leading his opponents. Michael Phelps would spring

## CHAPTER SIX – SWIMMING LESSONS

in the butterfly as his arms charged the water. He has great confidence. I am sure at times he was tired, but the victory was in view. He had a champion state of mind that would not allow him to fail. His presence was known due to his history of triumphs. He knew how to swim. He knew how to press through. In life, you do not stop when the Enemy is on your heels. You cannot stop! Keep swimming. Keep kicking. Continue moving forward with the victory in view.

The time will come when you must swim against the opposition and strong currents. However, you must learn to be triumphant when you feel you are drowning. Be vigilant. Be strong. At times, you will feel you are swimming against the tide, which can be hard and discouraging, but you will come through victoriously. In the midst, remember these powerful words:

> *Sometimes you have to swim against the tide, at times you have flown in the face of opinion, sometimes you have to decide which side, that you are going to take, there are moments when taking a stand is the only right thing to do, even if it goes against other plans, in the end, that's just the way it is, don't go getting it twisted, don't think what you're doing is wrong, just because you're not following the other fishes, swimming in life's pond, sometimes you have to be unique, sometimes you need to show your individuality on occasions, you have no choice, you have to make your voice heard in the end, that's just the way it is, so don't go getting it twisted, don't think what you're doing is wrong, just because you're not following the other fishes swimming in life's pond.*[v]

## Chapter 7

# The Broken Pieces Saved My Life

Like the night–quiet, solemn, and calm, grace has a way of peeking through and casting peace in the place of chaos. Grace has a way of showing up just in time to save you from what could be death. Grace has a way of squeezing in and savoring the little bit that is left to sustain you. Grace creeps quietly and gently, but you will know it is there. You will feel it; you will hear it. Why? That which came to kill you didn't work. That which came to break you down and destroy you didn't work. That which came to continuously remind you that you would never be anything but a statistic didn't work. That which came to rip you apart and discourage you, ended up catapulting you to the place you dreamed of going, though you didn't think you could get there.

Grace shows up to show you just what the favor of God is. Grace is the thread that knits everything together but doesn't always make sense. Grace takes all the tarnished, bruised, fragmented, cracked, shattered, and broken pieces of your life and makes a beautiful canvas to show you where you came from and how you look now. On this canvas, you will see flaws, mistakes, regrets, addictions, crises, and the ugly pieces you tried so hard to keep hidden. You have finally come to realize it was not you who kept those broken pieces of your life hidden. It was grace that held all the unpleasant and ugly broken pieces you were ashamed of together to keep you from breaking. I just screamed, "Thank You, Jesus!"

You did not break. You survived. You didn't die in the process. You got better. Take a moment and reflect on those moments. You are still here. You may not have it all together, but you have managed to keep it together. That's grace. Grace is the hand that held your life together. Grace is the influence that held back the devastating storm in your life, which wanted to destroy you and make you sink. Grace kept you strong when the Enemy came to take you to a place of no return in your deepest of seas. Got it? Now picture this. Grace canceled it. Grace nullified it. Grace abolished it! Grace is that powerful! Grace is your superpower.

Sadly, for some, life is a risky sea. Sometimes people find themselves barely making it safely to the shore on broken pieces while fighting through afflictions, loss, the unknown, tragedies, and life's stressors. Let me share something with you that you may not know. God's love for us exists in every situation we face. His love is constant. It's persistent, endless, and everlasting. Aren't you grateful for grace?

Many times in my life, I fought to hold on tightly to life itself. You see, life will try to squeeze every ounce of breath from you without notice. Life slaps you in the face with situations you can't dismiss; you are forced to deal with them. At times, we can't fix the problems, and it is scary, but we must pray incessantly. I fought to remain above all the junk and rubbish beneath me that thrived on entangling me. I was not going to lose the tight hold I was destined to keep. Thank God, I kept my grip.

## Don't Let Go

I declare you will keep your grip. You might feel letting go is the easy way out. It's not! Take a moment and picture in your mind you are holding onto a rope that begins to burn your hands. Bruises and burn marks are all over your hands, and you are in pain. The grip starts to feel much more intense and unbearable. Your hands get sweaty, and your strength starts to fade, so you let go. You let go because you don't feel the pain was worth it. We let go because we can't deal with the pain or sacrifices required to accomplish what we truly desire.

## CHAPTER SEVEN – THE BROKEN PIECES SAVED MY LIFE

Life has a way of teaching us to try harder. Life has a way of teaching us to maintain our stance even when the voices in our heads become louder and louder, suggesting we quit. Don't you quit! I learned that with God's grace, I have already surpassed what wanted me to sink. I have already figured out the distractions and decoys designed to make me remain in a sunken place. My friend, you must figure out–with prayer and discernment–the one thing or perhaps several things in your path that are there to defeat you.

When I think about God's grace, it reminds me of Paul's story. Paul endured a storm, and it appeared as if two seas were tussling and opposing each other. The winds were blowing and the waves thrashing. It was a battle at sea. The ship broke because of the violence of the waves and the front of the ship was stuck in a reef. Everyone aboard the ship saw the shore ahead of them, but the question they pondered was "What do we do now?" Paul had to make a hard decision to survive.

> Paul said to the centurion and to the soldiers… Except these abide in the ship, ye cannot be saved. And the soldiers' counsel was to kill the prisoners, lest any of them should swim out, and escape. But the centurion, willing to save Paul, kept them from their purpose; and commanded that they which could swim should cast themselves first into the sea, and get to land: And the rest, some on boards, and some on broken pieces of the ship. And so, it came to pass, that they escaped all safe to land. (Acts 27:31, 42-44)

Don't allow life to throw you overboard. If it gets strong and tough, grab whatever you can find within reach to stay above water. Let us probe deeper into this story of Paul. In the 27th chapter of Acts, Luke shares how the apostle Paul and his shipmates endured a storm while on a journey to Rome. They were in the deepest of waters, and they were in the hands of God. What I love about God is He always has a plan in place to save us. His personality is fascinating. Look at this picture. The ship is broken into pieces—not to abolish them, but to save them. The broken pieces are symbolic. Think deeper.

When reading this thought-provoking story, I found it powerful that some of the shipmates made it safely to shore on planks and other wreckage from the broken ship. They came in on broken pieces. Some even had the grace to swim the distance to safety. Some were graced to float. You may be coming in on broken pieces; it is okay. Just come. This is a sure sign that our great God has His hands on you. Friends, God has prepared great plans for your life, and the Enemy is so mad at you. So what?! Adopt a *so-what* attitude! You must see the Enemy's plan so you remain afloat. Don't you dare sink. Situations will become stormy, cloudy, and boisterous in your life, but grip the one thing that will sustain you and keep you from drowning. Life's challenging episodes build and mold us; grace lets us remain and not fall.

## Save Yourself!

Can you imagine being on the journey to Rome when a big storm suddenly brews? The storm was described in Acts 27:14 as "a tempestuous wind called Euroclydon." Imagine being in a sea of never-ending water fighting not to drown. Not to mention, you can see the land way in the distance but the deepest of waters separate you from it! It takes grit and determination to hold on to the planks, rubbish, and pieces of debris to save your life. I can't imagine the terrifying feeling of possibly losing my life in the sea filled with others who are fighting the same fight. Jesus! The fear and anxiety of it all cause desperation to set in. The goal is to get to shore. You have no time to save anything but yourself. That is the harsh reality. There will be a time in your life when you must be selfish to save yourself. I repeat—save yourself!

What a journey at sea. Paul was not a sailor, but he knew God. The centurion gave instructions in an effort to save Paul, which benefited saving all on board the ship. That's the favor of God. Please read and study this story in its entirety; it is powerful. I can visualize some shipmates throwing things overbroad. I imagine the ship beginning to sink.

## CHAPTER SEVEN – THE BROKEN PIECES SAVED MY LIFE

In life, you must let go of some things to live. Our God will demand you release the odds and ends you thought you could not survive without. Life can be stormy. It can be up and down. When life is breaking apart, salvage the one piece that gives you strength. Be determined to reach the shore, even if it's on a broken piece. You will get to your blessed destination because of God's grace.

It is a fact that the Enemy's plan was to drown you in the deepest of waters, but you are still alive. God did not allow you to drown. The broken pieces saved you. Paul prayed for a safe, peaceful journey, but he had a sudden jolt of life's harsh realities. His situation could have ended differently, but grace covered him. Broken pieces are often despised and regarded as useless, but sometimes, they are the very things God uses to rescue us. In our brokenness, God can minister and speak to our souls. Let Him minister to you. Learn through your broken moments that God is the One Who mends.

Grace is the residue of tragedy that allows you to get where you need to go despite the tempestuous winds in life. When the ship was broken and destroyed, Paul instructed his shipmates to grab a piece of the

> *You did not break.*
> *You survived.*
> *You didn't die.*
> *You got better.*

broken vessel and sail to shore. The wood floats even if the ship isn't together. They weren't supposed to make it. It seemed humanly impossible. My friend, you too were not supposed to make it. But you did! You too were supposed to be lost in the deep, untamed, and boisterous sea called life. However, the broken pieces saved your life. Be thankful for God's amazing grace that escorts us to safety. And all who were on the ship with Paul made it to land safely.

The winds of grace are always blowing; all we need to do is raise our sails.[vi]

## Chapter 8

# My Little Sister

It was a lovely Friday afternoon–quite chilly I might add; however, it had been a good day. I had the opportunity to speak with a young lady. She was exquisitely beautiful and highly intelligent. Who would have thought she had such a deep, dark past? You would have never known just by looking at her. Her smile, beauty, and a halo of happiness overshadowed her. She had big, bright, warm eyes, long brunette hair, and a face you could never erase. Her face was perfect; her eyes shined as brightly and boldly as the sun. Her welcoming spirit was unforgettable, so sweet, calm, and peaceful it was. When she opened her mouth to speak joyfulness and pride were in her voice; it was a sound of victory. She had gained a new zest for living. She was indeed excited about life and had a story to tell.

Life for her was now worth living. It took on a whole new meaning. Waking up to a life of freedom was pure joy. Bliss! She has a testament of triumph. She is an overcomer defeating each aching, disappointing, and dark experience she endured. She did not know those experiences would be the very things that painted the picture others looked at in awe. We have heard this statement a thousand times I'm sure, "You never know what a person has gone through." Well, it is true. We don't. People speculate, judge and question… We do not know other people's experiences until they share their testimonies. And when they do, we don't often understand unless we have been there ourselves. Honestly, we have no clue the level of pain, frustration or the weight others carry because we can't judge by the outside.

Many wounded hearts and scarred lives are masked behind fake smiles and words of comfort, "I'm good." "I'm okay." "I'm Cool." "Nothing is wrong." Behind the masks are broken hearts, silent cries for help, and someone clinging on for dear life. We can sympathize but we can never fully understand unless we have walked in someone's shoes.

Life can be chaotic and complicated for many reasons and at different seasons. We all can testify from different places and emotions of the challenges life has brought us. I see now that my journey has been rewarding as I reflect on what could have been or should have been. Yet, grace has been unmatched in my life. Grace has shown up when I could have easily checked out or given up. I'm sure you can say the same. When you pause and listen to life lessons from others, it is easy to see how merciful God is. My stories, your stories are not that bad after all. Hearing others' stories moves you from a place of pity and complaining to a deep place of gratitude. You begin to appreciate life at a whole new level. Life is good! It is no longer as complicated as the Enemy made it seem. I've come to realize God permits situations in our lives so we can gain new perspectives, new hope, and new meaning for life.

## Functioning in Dysfunction

The young lady I met wanted to be better. She was a teenager in an unhappy space; something had to give. She had no love in her life to push her to a place of change. She only had herself. Life was not simple for her. Pause right here. Give someone grace. You could have been her. Okay, carry-on reading. She was okay in her pain. Her pain felt natural. Again, she was functioning in dysfunction. She embraced her pain as if it were a friend. That was a lie but her truth–the truth but deception.

My pain and yours connect us. We connect when we stop to consider another's journey. I did not experience exactly what this young lady went through, but I could relate to her pain. I could also relate to being in a dark place, but in this case, I felt her pain was deeper given she was only 16 years old. At 16 years old, one usually lives a life of consistency and protection. At least, this should be the norm. When I was that age, my mother and father were both in the home. My parents were my anchor, and my home was one of peace and love. I had no complaints other than those of typical teenagers. I lived well by God's grace. Not everyone comes from a stable home. Everyone hasn't been saved all his/her life. Therefore, stop judging. Frankly, everyone does not know God. The person may not have yet met the Savior. But we must pray he/she will be introduced to the One Who makes all things new and whole. Completely!

- ♥ Her story: pain, heroin, homelessness, and suicide
- ♥ Her sustainer: grace
- ♥ Her point of reference: her little sister

Sadly, this young lady had such a dark past. It was one the average person would be ashamed of. Yet, she found strength in reflection. She smiled while telling her story. She had the kind of smile that could force a smile in return. Her life, indeed, is now a testimony of victory. How loving is our Father! He sustains the little left within us to pull us out of the darkness that could doom us to death. God's grace is greater than we could ever envision.

> For from His fullness we have all received, grace upon grace. (John 1:16)

We would completely erase our pasts if we could, but unfortunately, it is what it is. I recall First Lady Michelle Obama sharing, "Your story is what you have, what you will always have. It is something to own." At times, it raises its head and creeps up on our heels. We can grow from our pasts and others can glean and learn from our life lessons. We must be willing to share the good and the bad stuff. All of it! The awesome part of our lives is that God restores and redeems every piece of us that needs to be fixed, even those areas that require full replacements. He has us! Our great God takes the broken and ugly seasons of our lives and places them upon Jesus. Grace indeed. What a beautiful exchange! How awesome is it that Jesus loves us so much He replaces the shortcomings, embarrassments, times we knew better and did not do better, with good for His glory! Oh, how He loves us. I have so much gratitude, and my heart continues to stand in awe of Him.

*We would erase our pasts if we could, but it is what it is.*

We've all heard the saying to never judge a book by its cover. In this case, I did. And have you been that judge too? The look of this young lady was untarnished, nothing but beauty. I didn't know my giving encouragement would bless me to understand deeply that everyone has a "from." Yes, we all come from somewhere, someplace. It may not be pretty, but we all have that place. Some of us leap from that place when given the first chance to escape; others stay longer than they need to.

Her home life was not the best environment. It was often dark, and there was an undertone of sadness and confusion that hovered over her. She eventually figured it out. She learned why her home life was dark and gloomy. There was no faith. There was nothing positive to sustain her or fill the void. She felt pain. There was always a feeling of loneliness and sadness. She learned that the person who was supposed to be her teacher, example, and role model knew not God. Her mother was an atheist.

## Abnormal

She began asking herself questions. Am I normal? If this is normal, then I don't want to live. The suicide attempt failed. The darkness got deeper. The pain got more real. When she awoke in a hospital, she continued to fall into the depths of the unknown she explained. I call it depression. Not feeling better or healthy enough to move forward. Yet, unbeknownst to her, grace was her sustaining factor. She didn't even know what grace was, but she knew she was yet alive to live a new and different life. Can you relate to almost dying but getting the chance to live again? Can you relate? I mean even spiritually, emotionally, or psychologically.

She sank deeper. She explained the drugs made her sick, but she could not go without them. When she tried to stop taking the drugs, she got even sicker, so she continued to use them until she felt normal. Normal. Isn't it remarkable how the Enemy will set you up to make you feel normal when you are already in obscurity? He gets a kick out of beating you down and is thrilled to see you suffer. A trick! A sick pattern of deception. The Word gives us the resume of the Enemy.

> The thief cometh not, but for to steal, and to kill, and to destroy: I come that they might have life and that they might have it more abundantly. (John 10:10)

The mangy Enemy is a thief. I get what she was going through. I felt her anguish. I understand how the Enemy is a crafty thief. His complete strategy is to rob us all of the lives God has for us. The Enemy is only doing his job. There is a powerful piece written by my anointed friend Lorenda Barber and her dear friend Tasha Bellamy. These two friends' passionate writings reminded me of how the Enemy works in the minds of people. The piece also shines a light on the Enemy's agenda to mentally and physically break a person.

> *Your love of self-intimidates him. Healing terrifies him. Growth confuses him. Be reminded that your light continues to shine despite him. His inability to break you stifles him. You must move forward anyway... grace declares! The enemy will keep watching you grow and glow. Remember that the elevation game of God is strong. The ditch the enemy dug; he can have it. Please excuse the dust we left at his front door. We won't be back. Gone! Mentally and physically! Grace undergirds the strength needed to release that which gripped us. Sadly, we know people won't understand it now, but soon one day, while looking up from their sunken*

> *place, they will get it too. Our prayer is that you realize that it is God's grace that also woke you up this morning. We get it but when will you!*

I get it! Thank you, ladies, for allowing the Holy Spirit to write these words. Meditate on this piece; it's the truth, my friends.

He is our Enemy but be reminded–you can have the abundant life God has promised. We must fight for our deliverance! Without a doubt, God is greater than the Enemy. He tiptoes into our world with diminutive things to stop us. Be careful. Be watchful. Whatever we are facing, we must be confident there is absolutely nothing too hard for our great God. With the strength of our great God, we are not suffocated by what we go through. Life was suffocating the young lady! But you can be blessed in the midst of pain. You can triumph right where you are if you declare the Enemy defeated. Speak your victory out loud. Your words give legs to your destiny. What are you trying to do? What are you trying to create? The very words you speak could catapult you into your future success or deem you defeated. Sometimes you must take a moment and ask yourself some heartfelt questions. Self-inventory is key. Self-assessment is powerful.

## Grace the Sustainer

Grace has a way of getting us back to a safe place. In spite of all the bad, grace shows us what wholeness looks like. The ultimate goal in life is wholeness. Grace introduces you to the Sovereign God.

I asked her questions. What changed it all? What was your point of reference that completely caused you to make a 180-degree turn? What was the thing that caused you to be better than yesterday? Her answer, "My little sister." She said, "When I looked into my sister's eyes, I didn't want her to become me. I thank God for my little sister."

> *Happiness cannot be traveled to, owned, earned, worn, or consumed. Happiness is the spiritual experience of living every minute with love, grace, and gratitude.*[vii]

You are halfway through this book. I invite you to take time to meditate, take deep breaths, and make a few notes on what you have read that pierced your heart and caused you to think about your life lessons before you continue to the deep end.

_____
_____
_____
_____
_____
_____
_____
_____
_____
_____
_____
_____
_____
_____

"My trust in God flows out of the experience of His loving me, day in and day out, whether the day is stormy or fair, whether I'm sick or in good health, whether I'm in a state of grace or disgrace. He comes to me where I live and loves me as I am." —**Brennan Manning**

Let's swim further…

## Chapter 9

# Grace Period

God has instructed us all to do a certain task or go to a certain place. If we let the truth be told, there are times in our lives we do not want to heed the voice of God. We simply refuse! However, we will face the consequences, good or bad. Our disobedience might be due to selfishness, hurt, fear, resentment… maybe stubbornness. When I was disobedient, unfaithful, and perhaps a bit unloving, God continued to love me regardless of me. Regardless! God shows us so much grace at times when we simply don't deserve it. I love Him so much just for that.

> The compassionate and gracious God, slow to anger, abounding in love and faithfulness. (Exodus 34:6)

God is compassionate and graceful. Absolute joy is knowing God is the One Who ultimately saves all of us from destruction. Joy is knowing God shows grace to those who show no grace, mercy, or love. His grace is that awesome. And when we fail, His grace picks us right up, dusts us off, and sends us forward. I am incredibly grateful for the grace bestowed upon me when I may have otherwise been out of the will of God.

Grace period–the period given after your due date has passed.

Sometimes God instructs us to finish, act, show up or start a task but we fail. This is when we need a God-given grace period. A grace period is God demonstrating His hand of love when situations could have resulted in something other than for our good. In the natural, if I don't pay a bill within the grace period, my car is repossessed, and I get a negative hit on my credit report. The consequence of not taking care of responsibilities has a negative impact, and the repercussion can affect you later. You take a loss. Life can turn on a moment's notice without your permission. A grace period is God's forgiveness lending you another opportunity to get it right. What a blessing.

## Jonah's Reluctance

God does not speak hypothetically. He speaks accurately. He speaks the truth. God knows exactly what will come to pass. Our response to His obedience keeps us safe and secure no matter what the situation looks like. When God makes a request, the answer should always be yes. There are times when yes doesn't feel good, so we do not comply. Saying yes does not always feel comfortable. That is the reality. But grace has a way of reminding us that it is because of the Lord's mercy we are not consumed. His mercy is new and beautiful every morning. Do you remember when God instructed Jonah to go to a place he didn't want to go?

> Go to the great city of Nineveh and preach against it, because its wickedness has come up before me.
> (Jonah 1:2, NIV)

Nineveh was a wicked city full of sin and cruelty amongst the people. Why would anyone want to go there? People were killed, beheaded, tortured, disfigured, forced to live like animals, and treated as prisoners. Yet, God wanted Jonah to go preach against sin in the land. As for Jonah, he did not agree. Why would anybody want to help rebellious people who are unkind, wicked, mean, and malicious? Jonah must have been thinking, "Are we supposed to help them? How can I, in my humanity, help those who are so far gone? How is this humanly possible without losing myself?" Jonah was not trying to hear the voice of God. He was concentrating on the facts about that city. What can we learn from this story? Please read the entire story, it is insightful.

## CHAPTER NINE - GRACE PERIOD

- ♥ Lesson 1: Stay spiritual and focus on the assignment
- ♥ Lesson 2: Do not rely on your intellect
- ♥ Lesson 3: Do not study the facts of wickedness too long; study the Word
- ♥ Lesson 4: Remember that obedience has a victorious outcome
- ♥ Lesson 5: Remember the road you traveled and what it took for you to get free
- ♥ Lesson 6: Remember the definition of love according to the Word
- ♥ Lesson 7: There is a price to pay for disobedience.

What is the reason for these lessons? It is important not to lose focus when God has given you instructions. Losing focus will cause you to fight the wrong enemy. Be careful not to zone in to the casualties, the ruin, the hostages, or the damage done. Stay focused on your purpose. Don't forget Who God is. We breathe and live because of God. Don't focus on the effects of the war more than the Enemy. Don't allow the facts to play in your mind. As my dear sister, Lady Sharon Edwards would say, "Declare to the Enemy: 'This is the last time you play a movie in my head.'" The Enemy is behind it all. But God will preserve your sanity. Jonah had no intention of obeying anything God said. He focused more on the effects of wickedness. Unfortunately, his disobedience offered no help to those needing deliverance. Again, God said, "Go to Nineveh." Thank God for His grace period.

*Losing focus will cause you to fight the wrong enemy.*

What has been your Nineveh? Where is that grace period in your life, like Jonah? Where have you refused to go? Nineveh represents our great God's mercy and grace. For some of us, Nineveh is the place we resent going because we feel as if we are too good. Some deem Nineveh to be a place where the sinful are not deserving of the same grace they are given. Lest we forget our own sins. Is there a measure to sin? What do you do when God says, "Go to Nineveh"? Have you ever pondered the thought of God telling you no? How disturbed you would be!

> But Jonah rose up to flee unto Tarshish from the presence of the Lord and went down to Joppa, and he found a ship going to Tarshish: so he paid the fare thereof, and went down into it, to go with them unto Tarshish from the presence of the LORD. (Jonah 1:3)

Jonah did not care about this city of people. If Jonah had it his way, God would not love these people. Jonah failed to realize that he, too, had a grace period. See, we want mercy, but we fail to give it freely to others. We fail to see the big picture. God always has a plan for our lives, which hinges on our obedience to Him. We could be right on the verge of an enormous blessing, but disobedience causes the delay. Running in the opposite direction gets us nowhere. That's the part most people need to recognize.

## Run to Him

Rather than running from God, turn back. Run to and for Him. And do it quickly! Jonah ran from God. His disobedience to God landed him in an uncomfortable position. It put him in four places out of God's will. Jonah went to Joppa, into the ship, into the sea, and into the belly of a fish. While in the belly of the fish for three days, there was nastiness, spoil, foul smells, and profane darkness that had him mangled in the deepest of seas–alone. He was in a place where he could see his mistakes and think. He found himself in Nineveh, another lower part of life unbeknownst to him. His debt was past due. His grace period was extended. Thanks to God, Jonah realized his grace period with God and prayed a heartfelt prayer to Him.

## CHAPTER NINE - GRACE PERIOD

> In my distress, I called to the LORD, and he answered me. From deep in the realm of the dead I called for help, and you listened to my cry. You hurled me into the depths, into the very heart of the seas, and the currents swirled about me; all your waves and breakers swept over me. I said, 'I have been banished from your sight, yet I will look again toward your holy temple.' The engulfing waters threatened me, the deep surrounded me; seaweed was wrapped around my head. To the roots of the mountains, I sank down; the earth beneath barred me in forever. But you, LORD my God, brought my life up from the pit. "When my life was ebbing away, I remembered you, LORD, and my prayer rose to you, to your holy temple. Those who cling to worthless idols turn away from God's love for them. But I, with shouts of grateful praise, will sacrifice to you. What I have vowed I will make good. I will say, 'Salvation comes from the LORD.' And the LORD commanded the fish, and it vomited Jonah onto dry land. (Jonah 2:1-10, NIV)

At this point, Jonah got it. He remembered the Lord and admitted his need. We might think God is against us, but that is not the case. Sometimes it is fear. Sometimes it is simply thoughts planted by the Enemy. The Enemy, that evil Enemy, distracts us from being great in God when we fail to be obedient. Our grace period is acknowledging God calling us to surrender to His voice and not the voices in our heads.

God could have allowed Jonah to die in his disobedience; however, He saved his life. Grace! "Don't fight wrong so hard until you also become wrong." Thank you, Dad! I will never forget these words you often spoke. One of your greatest assignments is going where you do not want to go and allowing God to use you to bring change and deliverance to others entangled in sin, pain, bondage, or turmoil. I know; it's a tough reality.

Situations will come in our lives to test everything we say we believe. A situation will come to try our faith. Our tests of obedience are sometimes designed so we can't rely on anything or anyone but God. I am confident that when you come out of the test, you will have experience. You will have greater faith, a greater conviction, a deeper anointing, and a testimony.

You must give a resounding yes to God. Allow the Word of God to move you to walk in obedience. Although it may seem difficult to do, God is with you; therefore, it is well, my friend, so carry on. In our acts of obedience, God wraps Himself around us and covers us when we are perfectly placed to be overtaken by ourselves or the Enemy. Do not sway or alter what God has instructed you to do. Your life depends on it. Thank You, Lord, for Your grace.

## Chapter 10

# Grace for Today

As a child, talking with my father was like talking with the president of the United States of America. You could not tell me otherwise. His was the best wisdom a father could give a young girl. While sitting in my parents' garage, we spent many days having random conversations about life and living. He made so much sense. He gave wisdom that made you think twice. It was the kind of wisdom that makes you think before you act or speak words into the atmosphere to cause your day to go left. I guess you could say, he was the father who taught you how to use words wisely because he knew words have creative power on the earth.

My father often told me that life was beautiful, but it was what you made it to be. You know that old saying, when life gives you lemons, make lemonade. I learned this early. Now that I am older, it makes so much sense. Life is full of twists and turns, and sometimes you must role with them and rely completely on God's grace to overcome.

Grace is the factor that makes each day of life easier. Each day is a gift. Live! You must learn how to live. Many folks just haven't figured this out. The word "live" seems so simple to say but can be challenging to put into action. Those life lemons, for some, remain incredibly bitter and are never used to add sweetness to their lives. One thing about life is you must find a way to appreciate each day you have the privilege to breathe, touch, smell, and hear, even while facing challenges.

Prayer distracts and cancels the thoughts the Enemy brings to shift our focus from the precious moments of a beautiful, promising day. I do not want to ignore the fact that life can be challenging and leave a sour, disheartening taste. However, we must not forget about the beauty God brings to our world. Most of us can testify to the many lemons in our lives that have gifted us with several treasured opportunities to make lemonade. By God's grace, we can experience the sweetness of life.

## A Greater Life

I asked my mom, "Mom, why is it difficult for people to live a greater life?"

Her response, "They don't want to live a greater life."

I said, "Really? That's a bit harsh."

She said, "Yes, most people on this earth are not living because they don't want to sacrifice what it costs to live a greater life, so they remain complacent in their present, uncomfortable state, which is their normal."

She continued, "Daughter, life will teach you how to live. Despite your tests, you must allow God to do a work within you."

I had no other words. I simply processed her share of wisdom at that moment. I regularly revisit nuggets of wisdom shared by my mother. My mother has a secret to living well, for she is living–truly living. Such wisdom comes from a woman who has been blessed to reach the golden years of 91. I always pay close attention and take heed to the wisdom she shares.

I remember a time when I was complaining to my father about not having enough money for something special I wanted to purchase: an outfit, of course. Quickly, my father responded and said, "Daughter, what do you have on today? Appreciate today and tomorrow will take care of itself." Those words from my father pierced me at that very moment to make me change my mind about what I needed that week.Here comes a Bible debate, I thought. Truth spoken! I received

CHAPTER TEN - GRACE FOR TODAY

a life-changing word that would shape my perception forever. Once my father spoke these words to me, immediately, I stated, "now that's deep." An eye-opening passage of Scripture. Here it is.

> Therefore, I say unto you, Take no thought for your life, what ye shall eat, or what ye shall drink; nor yet for your body, what ye shall put on. Is not the life more than meat, and the body than raiment? Behold the fowls of the air: for they sow not, neither do they reap, nor gather into barns; yet your heavenly Father feedeth them. Are ye not much better than they? Which of you by taking thought can add one cubit unto his stature? And why take ye thought for raiment? Consider the lilies of the field, how they grow; they toil not, neither do they spin. (Matthew 6:25-28)

Thank you, father, for teaching me at an early age the Scriptures of truth. Why worry when God has already proven to us He is our constant? He has never changed or forgotten us. He is the persistent presence that reminds us He is with us. We are breathing. We can smell and hear. We can taste.

## Grace for Today

Many people spend so much time pondering about tomorrow, but tomorrow will take care of itself. Sadly, for some, tomorrow may not come. COVID-19, a worldwide pandemic, has definitely shown us what it means to live in the moment and appreciate the gift of life. Live your life to the fullest today. Grace for today is fulfilling. Grace for today is a promise to us to live free of worry. It is having a mindset of being free, living life undeterred, and appreciating each moment as a gift, rather than complaining. It is learning to appreciate the simple things that make you smile and laugh. How much time have you wasted mentally processing, imagining, doubting, and dreaming about tomorrow without appreciating today? It is easy to check out of today and begin living in tomorrow. But doing so does not help you live your best life. Be present today. Our gracious God gives us just enough grace for that one day.

*Put your energy into positive living, not worrying.*

God has given us the power to choose. I love the analogy in Matthew 6:25-28 because it defines how God's grace protects and sustains the simplest parts of His creation. God's grace lets us know that He cares for the fowls of the air that neither sow nor reap, yet, survive. He will also feed and give us everything we need. Consider how the lilies of the field grow. They do not toil or spin, but they live. The scripture asks the question, "Are we not more valuable?" If we are, why do we worry about tomorrow?

We take power from our anxious minds by silencing voices that cause us to worry about tomorrow when God has given us the grace to live for today. Put your energy into positive living, not worrying. Fuel up on God's Word. As my father told me in our garage, make gallons of lemonade; do not accept those old lemons. My father told me to make life good by not accepting gloom, doom, sadness, or worry. The beauty of life is that we can soar in moments even when we don't feel we have enough. We soar by recognizing God as our sustainer. He gives us everything we need for the now. I have learned that is more than enough.

Here is an excerpt from a thought-provoking article that fits so passionately:

> *As a child and a young person, I sometimes used to wonder and worry about what it would be like to be in their position. What would I do, if I were faced with a similar choice between denying Christ and painful death? I doubted whether I would be*

## CHAPTER TEN – GRACE FOR TODAY

> *so bold in service of the Lord as these young men were; I feared rather that I would cave under the pressure. As I have grown older, however, I have come to realize two things. First, God has not promised to give us the grace to face all the desperate situations that we might imagine finding ourselves in. He has promised to sustain us only in the ones that he brings us into. He, therefore, doesn't promise that we will imagine how we could go through the fire for his sake, but he does promise that if he leads us through the fire, he will give us enough grace at that time. Like Manna, grace is not something that can be stored up for later use; each day receives its own supply. Do you like me have desires to live a life that is sweet and precious? A beautiful life. Each morning you awake be reminded that it is God's grace that allows your eyelids to open, your feet to hit the floor, and your mouth to open and say to God, I thank you Lord for this new day that was not promised to me. Live each day with zest, happiness, and peace that can only come from Our God. Life will present its challenges at times but know that with each challenge, grace is a favor that each of us is given. Grace is the fragrance for the current day that allows us the matchless chance to do over what you failed or didn't try yesterday.*[viii]

Living free from worry and trying to remain free is a continuous effort, but you must open your heart to do so. Live your life in happiness, understanding grace is the muscle that keeps you pushing. When we align ourselves with the Creator, we set ourselves up to ultimately be free, no matter how many sour lemons come our way. You have a choice today to make lemonade. There's grace for today.

## Chapter 11

# Between Dilemma and Deliverance

There comes a time when life presents a choice to move forward or remain where we are. The goal is not to stay stuck between dilemma and deliverance. You will have to make one of the most important decisions of your life. Your life choices, progress, and destiny depend on you making the right decision. Sometimes the circumstances surrounding that decision are challenging and overwhelming. It is easy to get discouraged when you're choosing to stay still but see little to no movement. Why do I use the word "movement"? Movement symbolizes faith that is necessary for progress. Sometimes life tells us there is no way out. That is what the Enemy wants us to believe. Reject the hype of the Enemy. Do not believe it.

Have you ever tried to move onward for peace and freedom but got stuck between dilemma and deliverance? Have you ever been so desperate to taste freedom but could not find it? The loneliest feeling is when you desire to be free, but freedom won't render itself to you. So do you move forward in faith or stand still and be overtaken? Do you know what it's like to stand on the edge of your promise and the verge of your breakthrough? You can taste it. You can feel it. You are that close to your prosperity. Freedom is nearby but you are faced with reality. It is what it is, but faith defies human logic. Faith is that force to change your reality. See yourself free until you are free. Seeing is faith.

Remember the Red Sea? Revisit this story in Exodus Chapter 14. It represents all the junk that causes you to stay stuck in your past. It represents fear over faith. It represents everything our great God does not represent. Sometimes we peek back when we're at the crossroads in our lives. Peeking causes confusion. Thoughts of yesterday mingled with the ever-present suggestions from the Enemy creates chaos. We remember the pleasure and tend to feast on its fulfillment for a moment. Then we muster up the courage to let it all go mentally to crave for freshness and a new life that is more meaningful. Believe and trust that God is the link to get you over. He is your ultimate source of strength, your guiding light. He has a proven track record. Why settle at the crossroads? Cross over.

Don't be paralyzed by the decision you ultimately have to make. It is inevitable. You must move now or later. I understand crossroads are difficult to maneuver but remember they are necessary for your total deliverance. And that depends on you moving forward. You must own this part of the crossroad. Simply put, your mindset has to change. It is God's will that you move to a new place mentally. This comes by transforming your mind and not allowing this world to make you conform to its designs and processes. In Scripture, Apostle Paul boldly instructs the believer:

> And be not conformed to this world: but be ye transformed by the renewing of your mind, that ye may prove what is that good, and acceptable, and perfect, will of God. (Romans 12:2)

The time will come in our lives when we, like the children of Israel, will encounter a Red Sea crossing. We will need supernatural interventions. We will, no doubt, need the hand of Jesus to rescue us from what could be a fatal ending. But grace, coupled with faith, says not so.

# CHAPTER ELEVEN – BETWEEN DILEMMA AND DELIVERANCE

## The Larger Purpose

One of my favorite narratives begins in Exodus Chapter 2 when Moses was born. His mother gave birth to him and hid him for as long as she could. She then created a floating basket and placed it in the Nile River. While he was floating on the river, he cried–as 3-month-old infants do so well! His older sister, Miriam, who was about the age of 7 or 8, watched from afar as her baby brother floated down the river. It just so happened that the Princess of Egypt, Pharaoh's daughter, was bathing in the river at the same time. What timing! She told one of her servants to retrieve the child from the river, and the servant did as the princess requested. When the servant brought the floating basket to the princess, she opened it and the cries of a hungry infant pierced her heart. She was filled with compassion for the child. She said, "This is one of the Hebrew children."

Miriam, having seen all this, made her way toward the princess with a renewed hope for her baby brother and said, "Should I get a nursing mother of the Hebrews to care for the baby?" The princess sensed the solution to her current challenge and said, "Yes!" Miriam went home to her mother to give her the news about the safety of her baby brother Moses and the need for him to be nursed. Can you imagine the new life that sprung up in the heart of this desperate mother? When the mother of Moses arrived, the princess said to her, "Take this baby and nurse him for me. I will pay you." Not only was this woman's baby boy saved, but now she would get paid to do what she would gladly do for free!

*Why settle at the crossroads? Cross over.*

This arrangement lasted until Moses was weaned. Afterward, the princess gave him the official name "Moses" saying, "I pulled him out of the water." Remember the meaning of the name; it would be prophetic of God's larger purpose for this child.

Moses was raised in the palace as a young child. He received a royal education, royal treatment, and royal nourishment. His worldview and experiences were royal but his empathy for the Hebrew plight did not vanish. Even though he was in the palace, he knew of the oppression his people suffered. This is evidenced by his reaction when he witnessed an Egyptian hitting a Hebrew. It did not matter how long he was in the palace; Hebrew was still in his DNA.

Moses killed that Egyptian and buried him in the sand. The next day, he went to the same area and saw two Hebrew men fighting. He questioned the context of the argument, and one spoke up and said, "Why? Who do you think you are? Are you going to kill me like you did the Egyptian?" Moses then realized his secret was out. In a way, it was a heads up because Pharaoh was plotting to kill him. Moses fled for safety. Along the way, he found a young lady named Zipporah whom he would later marry.

## CHAPTER ELEVEN - BETWEEN DILEMMA AND DELIVERANCE

While Moses was working for his wife's father, Jethro, shepherding his flock, he noticed a burning bush. As Moses got closer to the bush, he saw that it was burning, but it was not consumed. Physics says if something is on fire, compound molecules separate, and the object is destroyed. Not in this case! The bush was on fire, but it maintained its structure. It was all God. God then gave the bush vocal cords and called out, "Moses!"

Moses said, "I am here!"

God gave Moses instructions saying, "Take off your sandals. This is holy ground."

God reintroduced Himself to Moses as the God of Abraham, Isaac, and Jacob. He also explained that He had heard the cries of His people for deliverance and said, "I am sending you back to Pharaoh to bring My people out of Egypt."

## Crossroad

Now, within the context of the story, the original Pharaoh had died. His son was his successor and the reigning Pharaoh of Egypt. Remember, Moses was raised in the palace by the princess, which means Moses probably had frequent dealings with the new Pharaoh as a child. There must have been a relationship established at the palace. Moses was aware of the authority, personality, and history of this new Pharaoh. The relationship went from being familial while Moses was living at the palace to adversarial. Crossroad!

Moses gave God every excuse not to take on the assignment–from the inability to speak properly to his social status. God gave him several signs and eventually convinced Moses to go. Moses says, "What do I tell them when they ask about your name?"

> And God said unto Moses, I AM THAT I AM: and he said, Thus shalt thou say unto the children of Israel, I AM hath sent me unto you. And God said moreover unto Moses, Thus shalt thou say unto the children

> of Israel, the LORD God of your fathers, the God of
> Abraham, the God of Isaac, and the God of Jacob, hath
> sent me unto you: this is my name forever, and this is
> my memorial unto all generations. (Exodus 3:14-14)

God instructed Moses to draft his brother Aaron as the spokesperson due to Moses' insecurities. Moses and Aaron coordinated a leadership meeting with the elders of the Hebrews. The last verse in Exodus Chapter 4 says they bowed down and worshipped the Lord after hearing the words of comfort from Moses and Aaron.

The God of Israel instructed Moses and Aaron to tell Pharaoh to let His people go. God outlined the dire consequences of Pharaoh's disobedience. But Pharaoh refused and increased the workload of the Hebrews in retaliation for Moses and Aaron's audacious request. The Hebrew people began to grumble against Moses and Aaron due to the hardship placed upon them.

Moses went back to God concerned about what had happened. You do not bargain with God. Bargaining is not an option with Him. God sent the ten plagues upon the land of Egypt because Pharaoh did not release the Hebrews. The final plague God sent was the most severe; it ultimately cost all the families of Egypt their firstborn.

God gave instructions for the Hebrews to take the blood of a lamb and rub it on the doorposts of each home belonging to them. Once they did this, the angel of death would pass over every home with the bloodstain. When Pharaoh realized the firstborn sons of Egypt were dead, he kicked the Hebrew people out of the land. The Hebrew people left Egypt with silver and gold. Not only did they come out of bondage, but they left bondage with riches. Grace was before them, and their enemies behind them.

As the Hebrew people were leaving the land of the Egyptians, Pharaoh changed his mind and pursued them with his mighty military and chariots. The Hebrew people reached the edge of the Red Sea and began to grumble. Their oppression seemed to increase the closer they

## CHAPTER ELEVEN - BETWEEN DILEMMA AND DELIVERANCE

got to freedom. There were mountains on both sides of them, the Red Sea in front of them, and the Egyptians behind them. They were at a crossroad. They had nowhere to go but forward. When you are at a crossroad, there is no time to complain. You have no time to let your mind be consumed with negativity and what ifs. Some of the Israelites began to mumble and complain as if grace was not with them. This was a time when they needed to acknowledge God and Who He is when we need Him most. Grace intervened.

> Then they said to Moses, "Because *there were* no graves in Egypt, have you taken us away to die in the wilderness? Why have you so dealt with us, to bring us up out of Egypt? *Is* this not the word that we told you in Egypt, saying, 'Let us alone that we may serve the Egyptians'? For *it would have been* better for us to serve the Egyptians than that we should die in the wilderness." And Moses said to the people, "Do not be afraid. Stand still, and see the salvation of the Lord, which He will accomplish for you today. For the Egyptians whom you see today, you shall see again no more forever. The Lord will fight for you, and you shall hold your peace." And the Lord said to Moses, "Why do you cry to Me? Tell the children of Israel to go forward. But lift up your rod, and stretch out your hand over the sea and divide it. And the children of Israel shall go on dry *ground* through the midst of the sea. And I indeed will harden the hearts of the Egyptians, and they shall follow them. So I will gain honor over Pharaoh and over all his army, his chariots, and his horsemen. Then the Egyptians shall know that I *am* the Lord, when I have gained honor for Myself over Pharaoh, his chariots, and his horsemen." And the Angel of God, who went before the camp of Israel, moved and went behind them; and the pillar of cloud went from before them and stood behind them. So it came between the camp of

the Egyptians and the camp of Israel. Thus it was a cloud and darkness *to the one,* and it gave light by night *to the other,* so that the one did not come near the other all that night. Then Moses stretched out his hand over the sea; and the Lord caused the sea to go *back* by a strong east wind all that night, and made the sea into dry *land,* and the waters were divided. So the children of Israel went into the midst of the sea on the dry *ground,* and the waters *were* a wall to them on their right hand and on their left.

(Exodus 14:11-22, NKJV)

The Bible explains how God overthrew the Egyptians. What a powerful move of God! The plan of God will always trump the plan of the Enemy. The Red Sea parted with the simple movement of Moses' rod. Therein was the true authority God gave Moses. He had the faith to believe the water would move by the power of God, so he obeyed God. The rod was nothing more than a simple rod, but Moses' faith in its movement was miraculous; it demonstrated God's grace. Moses did not have the technology; he had faith. He was acquainted with the work of the Savior. We say we know God, but do we trust Him? Yes ☐ or No ☐

The waters divided and stood up as a wall of victory on each side making a pathway to freedom. God will always make a way for our escape. The grace of God graciously worked through Moses when he yielded himself as a willing vessel. He also found mercy with God. The children of Israel walked through on dry land. It was not muddy, damp, or wet land. It was dry land. Incredible! The grace of God led them through. This was one of their crossroad experiences, but grace went before them.

# CHAPTER ELEVEN – BETWEEN DILEMMA AND DELIVERANCE

## Covered and Protected

When you cannot understand why, rest in the assurance that God knows what is up next. He knows what is best for you, but you must believe it. You must say yes. Yes, I believe. I have faith. God delivered the children of Israel. He is the great deliverer.

No words can sum God up in totality. God is awesome! He permitted 7,254 feet and 169,100 square miles of water to divide itself and stand up in its vast power. I can imagine the sound of roaring deep waters as they obeyed God! God made the seas by the power of His word and the Red Sea had to obey His voice. The sea remained upright as a pathway of grace for the children of Israel to walk through. A wall of water was on the right and a wall of water on the left. How long did it take the children of Israel to walk through the Red Sea? Can you imagine their mindsets and how they felt when faced with the deep waters? And not to mention, the creatures in the sea, dead and living, did not harm them. Grace.

The children of Israel were led by a pillar of fire by night and a cloud by day. God covered them with His hand. The cloud covered them during the day and the pillar of fire allowed them to see at night. The cloud was the glory of God resting over His people as He ushered them with His hand of grace to the other side. I see the fire by night as a purifying metaphor to cover the people and protect them from any impurities or anything that may have impeded their progress. Covered and protected. The grace of God protected the children of Israel against the same enemies that oppressed them for over 400 years. This was generations of oppression. The curse of bondage, oppression and hatred would now be broken.

Immediately, when they all crossed, Moses looked back and saw that God allowed the enemies–Pharaoh's army–to drown in the Red Sea. Drown! And to think Pharaoh had the nerve to believe God would permit his army to also come through on dry land! The Egyptian army would be no longer. Moses looked back and was able to see the hand of God at work.

On the other side of your crossover is your purpose. It's everything you dreamed of. It's everything you imagined. It is every possibility waiting for you. Cross over! Do not look back. We cannot cross the seas of our lives in our might. God will part the waters for us. Take solace in the fact that grace leads the way.

Remember the goal. Don't stay stuck between dilemma and deliverance.

## CHAPTER 12

# GOD'S GLORY

It takes confidence, authority, and grace to fiercely position yourself in the midst of adversity. The way we go through, the way we respond, and what we choose to learn from the experience determine our outcomes.

When adversity knocks at our front door, we spend time questioning God by asking Him a plethora of questions:

- ♥ Why me?
- ♥ Why do I have to face adversities?
- ♥ Why did adversity come at this point in my life?
- ♥ What is this all about?
- ♥ How long will this test last?

I am sure you have been there. You have questioned God.

Finally, your life is well. You are in a good place. Suddenly, trouble comes. The vital question is are you up for the battle? The Word tells us the battle is not ours but God's. Do you believe it? We say we believe, but do we? I get it. We wrestle with our situations. Sometimes we get stuck in our thoughts trying to figure out the ways and whys of our situations. It won't work that way. It never does. Take solace in knowing trouble does not last always. Well, at least, this is what we pray for.

Fighting challenges in your own strength makes the road to victory a long and tedious one. Adversity will break you or make you. Adversity will build your faith muscles or cripple you. The journey will make you a victim or a victor. You choose. Adversity has a way of touching our lives differently. It takes courage and ambition to fight. Bear in mind the fight is not always with words or physical with fists and uppercut blows. Sometimes, the fight is in the mind. However, God graces us with the physical, emotional, and mental fortitude to win. Our confidence is in the road map He left us to conquer and withstand all we are up against. The road map is the Word of God. Every twist, turn, detour, setback, pitfall, and ambush is explained in the Word of God.

*In our adversities, we show the world Jesus is the King of all kings.*

God has set a way of escape before us. He has given us the strength to stand firm and unshaken when hit by adversity. Your faith in God will sustain you no matter what situation you are facing. Grace also has a way of lifting you out of the stuff that is designed to destroy you. Therefore, you must look through the lenses of faith and not your intellect or understanding. You must see yourself victorious. You are a conqueror! And more than!

Everything we encounter is for God's glory. In our adversities, we show the world Jesus is the King of all kings. God's hand of grace rescues us from the hand of the Enemy. We have seen God's track record. We will have distractions and problems. They are inevitable. Focusing on God instead of our problems keeps us in a place of peace. We have peace in knowing we are more than okay.

CHAPTER TWELVE - GOD'S GLORY

## Deborah the Warrior

Deborah was a fearless woman in the Bible. She was courageous and the Enemy's forces could not stop her. She was destined to be the woman God formed and fashioned her to be. She was the ultimate boss lady–the ultimate game-changer. She was indeed a woman of greatness. Greatness meaning, she was in a position of importance and significance. She was gifted with the natural and spiritual ability and determined to show the world how great her God was. Deborah was a woman of power. She had authority, control, and strength. Her magnificent qualities developed due to her obedience to God. She held a great position as a judge of Israel but who she was to God made her even greater.

Deborah had an amazing purpose to defeat the Enemy for God's glory. Her story is a demonstration of how God will be revealed, known, and acknowledged in your situation. It was God's amazing grace that aided in a supernatural battle. We see it in the book of Judges.

> And I will draw unto thee to the river Kishon Sisera, the captain of Jabin's army, with his chariots and his multitude; and I will deliver him into thine hand. And Barak said unto her, if thou wilt go with me, then I will go: but if thou wilt not go with me, then I will not go. And she said, I will surely go with thee: notwithstanding the journey that thou takest shall not be for thine honour; for the LORD shall sell Sisera into the hand of a woman. And Deborah arose, and went with Barak to Kedesh. (Judges 4:7-9)

"I will surely go with thee," Deborah said. She immediately reminded Barak that the battle they were about to enter was not about them. It was about Jesus. This battle was God's for His glory. Deborah made a bold statement, "The Lord will sell Sisera into a hand of a woman." Was Deborah speaking of herself? Was she the woman? She was incredible and bold lacking nothing. Grace was the undercurrent that pushed her to be the mighty warrior she was alongside Barak in the battle.

Let us be clear. When God instructs His children to carry out an assignment, it is not about us. It has not been about us, and it never will be. Of course, it is one of the most wonderful feelings in the world to be a vessel on behalf of God. Still, it is not about us. The feeling of being used by God is refreshing and the result of obedience is incredible. We must not forget that our great God gets the glory. It is all for Him.

The glory of God surrounds us.

> *The heavens declare the glory of God; the skies proclaim the work of his hands. (Psalm 19:1, NIV). What does that mean? It means he is shouting at us. He shouts with clouds. He shouts with blue expanse. He shouts with gold on the horizons. He shouts with galaxies and stars. He is shouting. I am glorious. Open your eyes. It is like this, only better if you know me.*[ix]

You must know God. You must open your heart to see His splendor and power. The glory of God is all that is beautiful about God. It is all that is magnificent, which shines through His character. It is seen amongst mankind and throughout the earth. God's grace helps us to do what honors God the most. It is grace that equips us with strength. We conquer and are not defeated. Isaiah 43:7 says God created us for His glory.

God's glory is seen on the earth in so many ways. It is displayed by His love, rivers, flowers, mountains, the beauty of the seas, and the depth of the oceans. It is shown through the wisdom God gave man to build and to create. Our gifts and talents are to show forth God's glory. God's wisdom is our intelligence and direction.

Deborah's fierceness was a demonstration to all around her that God was her focus. She was the mother of Israel and blessed with many gifts. She was a prophetess endowed with a prophetic gift. She had the ability to distinguish the mind and purpose of God and declare it to others. God trusted her to deliver His Word to whom it was given. God gave her the favor and responsibility to rule a nation. What a powerful purpose to be able to liberate God's people to a life of freedom! It takes a strong and balanced person to remain focused knowing the journey in freeing others is not about them, but all for the glory and honor of God.

> *God's grace helps us to do what honors God the most.*

Deborah was the fifth judge of Israel and the only woman judge. She sat under a palm tree called the "Palm of Deborah." This tree was a consecrated place where God visited her and under it, Deborah bestowed justice and mercy. She had the authority to care for a nation that had been in captivity for forty years.

## Oppression Is Real and Deadly

In the book of Judges, the children of Israel were oppressed by the unforgiving King of Canaan. One of the most disheartening feelings is being kicked down when you want to come up in life. God is not pleased when this happens to His children. We know this, and amazingly, some people still try to take advantage of God's grace. They take advantage because they continue to keep oppressed people in a low place. Physical oppression also takes root in the mind. It is a harsh reality, but it is true. Have you ever had to fight to survive? I mean fight. Fight to stand strong in your thoughts and keep your spirit lifted. It is a fight worth fighting!

The people's spirits were fragmented. They felt as if all hope for liberation was gone. Thank God, Deborah saw the needs of the people and acted. She called for a man named Barak through the prophecy of God. Deborah told Barak that it was God's will for him to lead her forces and deliver her country. Barak responded, "If you go, I will go." Understand that naturally, Deborah was the weaker vessel, but I believe she had the greater faith. Barak knew Deborah was a woman of favor, faith, and courage.

Deborah and Barak's army were only 10,000 men. The enemy had 100,000 men and 900 iron chariots. Can you imagine going up against 100,000 enemies? I cannot imagine.

> Some trust in chariots, and some in horses: but we will remember the name of the LORD our God.
> (Psalm 20:7)

When in trouble, remember the name of the Lord. It looked as if all odds were against them, but Deborah and Barak had God as their ally. With God's power, we can stand strong in the face of all that opposes us. Be not dismayed at the adversities you face when resisting the Enemy. God has gone before you.

During the battle, Scripture states the heavens opened; the earth trembled; heaven dropped; the clouds dropped water, and the mountains melted. A violent storm came. They fought from heaven. The stars (which represented angels) fought against the enemy, and the river swept them away. God sent an earthquake and a hailstorm that overtook the land and the enemies ended up in a river. I am laughing so loudly. God will change the outcome for us! God put *super* on the natural! He reached from heaven and caused *the elements* to fight on their behalf. When in trouble, see God's hand. It is in every situation. If you don't see anyone else, see God. He is there.

*God put* super *on the* natural!

Can you imagine Deborah and Barak standing on dry land, while on the other side the enemies are in a great hailstorm? That's just like God in our situations. Hell can be erupting over there but God has covered you where you stand. Deborah knew what it looked like, but she also knew God is ever faithful. It is important to know God

CHAPTER TWELVE - GOD'S GLORY

in ways we've never known Him before. Why? When the facts of your life say you are defeated, knowing God reassures you that greater is He who is in you than he that is in the world. God says it is already done. The fight is fixed. We win.

In this story of Deborah, I can see God's hand in the spirit. On that day, there was a war going on in the heavens between the forces of good and evil. There was something special about this woman. She acted in greatness and power. She was God's mouthpiece and Barak respected her authority.

Barak knew Deborah had a strong relationship with God. He knew going against her was like opposing God Himself. She served as the eyes and ears of God and the anointing of God was on her. God put confidence in the hearts of 10,000 men to fight the oppressors. Don't worry about how many enemies are before you. Trust God. The enemies in your life will smile in your face while hoping passionately for your failure and plotting against you. However, no weapon formed against us shall prosper! Weapons may form; deadly words may be spoken, but the plots of evil will not work.

## There Is a Lesson in It

Sometimes God must take us to unfamiliar places where He will be revealed and glorified. Battles and adversities are sometimes designed specifically for us to solely depend on God. There is a lesson in it. On the other side, your faith will rest at another level with a deeper anointing, and you will have a powerful testimony. God never leaves experiences empty. This is the part I like about this story. The captain of the enemy's army, Sisera, thought he was getting away from the Israelites and death. He jumped off his chariot and ran on foot. This man of war had terrorized Israel for years, but God has an all-seeing eye. He sits high, but He looks low. Please remember what you are wrestling with.

> For we wrestle not against flesh and blood, but against principalities, against powers, against the rulers of the

> darkness of this world, against spiritual wickedness in high places. (Ephesians 6:12)

The Enemy employs immense pressure in the high places. The Enemy has a plan, but God has a better plan and a purpose. Look at what the enemy did. Captain Sisera ran to the tent of Heber. At the beginning of the story, Deborah told us God was going to deliver Sisera into the hands of a woman. Let me introduce you to Jael. She was a woman who specialized in tentmaking. Jael went into the tent where Sisera was. Look at the facts of Jael:

> Jael went out to meet Sisera and said to him, Come, my LORD, come right in. Don't be afraid. So he entered her tent, and she covered him with a blanket.
> (Judges 4:8, NIV)

Sisera asked Jael for some water because he was thirsty. Jael didn't just give him water; she gave him milk. Cunning, she knew milk would help him go to sleep. He told her to stand at the door and if anyone came and asked for him say he was not there. Jael stood at the door. While she was standing, she got a nail and a hammer. She waited patiently until Sisera went to sleep. Then, she smote the nail right through his temple with the hammer. He died.

- ♥ Jael had a plot and a plan
- ♥ In the midst of adversity, you must have a plan
- ♥ Prayer will give you a plan
- ♥ Fasting will give you a plan
- ♥ Being quiet will give you a plan

This woman helped save Israel. Now, I am not telling you to kill your enemies. However, you can silence their evil with the Word of God.

## Chapter 13

# Still Waters

Allow yourself to be vulnerable to the disappointments you have experienced so you can embrace the genuine emotions they produce. Heal rather than remain numb, which can eventually result in a breakdown that leaves you in pain and isolation. Disappointment can cause you to lie to yourself. You disregard your true emotions with subtle deception because you feel you are okay when you are not. Admit it. Having said that, I should also say sometimes we are okay.

Check your emotions by not allowing them to lie to you. Do not let pride sit in the seat of honesty. What does that mean? Pride can be a strong spirit that persuades you to say you are okay rather than confessing you are not. It's okay to say, "I'm not good today." You have allowed yourself to be numb, which is the counterfeit of hurt. At times, we tend to say we are okay for the sake of appearance and acceptance; this is another form of pride. Be careful!

Disappointments cause hurt. Hurt produces hurt toward others if not dealt with. The sad old saying remains true today, "Hurt people hurt others." Past hurt becomes a vicious cycle damaging others who use it as a weapon. The weapons birthed from disappointment are frustration, bitterness, unforgiveness, anger, and depression. If disappointments are not dealt with, they will repeatedly tumble into your present perception.

Disappointments often show up in our character, causing us to act out. During these times while acting out, many realize they have a problem and finally admit their disappointments. Give yourself permission to admit you are disappointed. It is okay to vent the truth so you can move on in the right way. The moral is we will all experience disappointment. However, how we process the disappointment determines our peace and freedom.

## Process and Unpack

In life, choosing your battles wisely is very important. Equally necessary is simply stating how you honestly feel; it does not have to be a battle. You deserve the freedom to express your emotions rather than hide them and act out later on. Wisdom is the principal thing. Wisdom determines the outcome of our situations, and we learn from each experience we encounter. Wisdom makes all the difference. Know when to close your mouth. Study to be quiet. I have been in situations where I lashed out inappropriately and then asked the question, "Where did all that come from?" It was bottled up inside because I did not express myself initially. I only did so when something triggered it. Those triggers can cause harsh, inappropriate, overreactions. Hence, you should know your triggers. Know what upsets you. It is vital.

*You can choose not to be offended.*

It is beneficial to express your disappointment and move on. It was beneficial for me. However, as I grew older and matured in Christ, I learned I could take all my frustrations and disappointments to God alone. I ran across Luke 17:1, a power scripture that says, "Offense will come." Wow! The Word said it. We will be offended and insulted. And with offense comes disappointments. In this life, we will experience offense on many levels. But you can choose not to be offended. You can choose not to be disappointed. Is it fair to say you can choose to feel your emotions by embracing them in order to move on? Process and unpack your emotions.

You should also look within and ask yourself why. Why am I disappointed? Many times, we don't even know why we are mad or upset. Our emotions are in an uproar. What is at the root of the way you feel?

I praise God for the Word. I encourage you to run for cover in the Word of God, which is stillness. It lifts you from what could be your quitting point to a place of pure peacefulness. By grace, we take refuge and courage to get to the root of issues. Get to the root of your stuff if you want to heal and be better. It takes time to dig deep within yourself. Getting to the root can be a long process, but it's worth the digging. A lot of ugliness is in the digging, but it is necessary if you want to heal.

## Being Vulnerable

While writing this chapter, I was talking to a son in the Lord about being vulnerable. He said something so clearly to me: "You can have peace in vulnerability." I paused and meditated just for a moment. Then I screamed, "Yes!" It sounds odd, but it is the truth. Being vulnerable allows you to face the thing that wants you to hide and scream. Being vulnerable may not be negotiable to you but consider it. When you become vulnerable, you take the power away from the Enemy. You are not letting the Enemy buffet you by reminding you of your disappointments. You tell the Enemy "Yes, it happened. I've dealt with it. I have surrendered it to God, and I'm moving on."

We bury disappointments and allow them to stay dormant. Please deal with the pain from it and rid yourself of the residue. The Enemy gets a kick out of this. He laughs. We tuck disappointments away in the back of our minds thinking we have disposed of them for good. But more often than not, they show their ugly heads to fight! When this happens, we find ourselves wrestling with our thoughts because we were not vulnerable.

In our times of disappointment, we are refreshed by the Word. The living Word of God takes the sting out of the hurt and pain. It graces us with the strength to move onward instead of sinking deep into our sad, emotional state of disappointment and self-pity

Truth and disappointment are inevitable. There is no escaping. There is a calm in the word of God. A stillness that only God can render. Our heavenly Father will encourage you and pour His grace on you when you feel broken and tired from the weight of life's situations. God takes the sting out of the most painful experiences that were crafted to wipe you out, literally. Take a deep breath and say out loud, "I thank God for grace." (Do you feel better? The release is refreshing.)

*Understand that being vulnerable does not mean you are weak.*

Grace covers your heart and mind. When I am disappointed, I picture the hand of God over my heart and mind. Just when I am about to give up is when grace shows up as my defense. Trust God on your journey. Talk to Him when it appears His Word is not working in your life. Be honest and ask yourself, "Do I believe in the Word?" Friends, the Word of God is real. It works if you believe. Occasionally, we will get weak but don't lose your faith.

It is important to understand that being vulnerable does not mean you are weak. You have the right to express your feelings. It is okay to be open. Being open releases the part of you the Enemy wants to keep tied down. Sometimes we refuse to share because we think we will be rejected or looked down upon as insignificant and victims. I get it.

Fear of disapproval will not allow you to expose the part of you that is hurt and disappointed. And it is okay if the other person will not accept your truth or hear and admit his or her part in it. Remember forgiveness and moving on are not for the other person; they are for you. There is freedom in moving on. We feel that not being vulnerable keeps us safe, which to some extent is true, but it holds us in bondage.

## Pause and Reflect

Take a moment to pause and reflect. What are your thoughts? We have heard this saying for years: "Chose your battles." I wholeheartedly believe this thought; however, at times, confronting is a good way to release those pent-up feelings. Have a mature conversation. Talk about it! Confronting does not have to be confrontational.

Have you ever felt like you needed space, a time-out from everyone and everything? You say: "Give me 50 feet. I need a minute to process. I am simply not the only one! And I still love the Lord. I need a moment to get it together. I need a moment to get myself together. My goal in life is to see Jesus. Give me 50 feet to deal with me, so I can be kind and true to others."

Now that you have exposed your truth and have allowed yourself to be vulnerable, it is necessary to be quiet. Now is the time to be extremely careful and not allow the Enemy to come in and cause you to throw a pity party around the truth you just shared. He is a master strategist at making one have regrets. The Enemy looks for every way to create confusion in our lives, so we can feel a plethora of emotions.

I can remember a sensitive time in my life when I was disappointed. It was a painful disappointment, the type you cannot talk about until you are ready. I needed more than 50 feet; I needed 100 feet–seriously. The disappointment I experienced wanted me to raise my fists. Someone I thought was a dear friend misused my heart. I found myself holding her hostage to the pain she made me feel. We tried to talk about it, but she was not willing to be honest, to be open, to be vulnerable. Why? It was an embarrassment on her part, and pride was winning. I was so disappointed to the point I felt justified walking by her and not speaking. I felt justified in allowing my presence to dominate her. Who did I think

I was? I was lost in pride by feeling I was right. Disappointments will cause you to stray from the path of God. Disappointments will cause you to walk in error. I trusted her–at least–I thought I could. We shared so many things about God, life, family, food, and we laughed often.

I refused to talk to her, and she refused to admit the truth or apologize. That's all I wanted–an apology. Emotions were on parade. My actions demonstrated meanness; I wanted her to experience that same hurt I felt. I felt her love for me, but she allowed the Enemy to attack her character. It was my opportunity to show her the real love of God. But the God I serve and testify about boldly was not being represented well. Agape love was not on the scene.

I could feel the shame and hurt on her because she was afraid to admit or apologize to me. And remember pride–it was her ally. I was also sitting in a seat of pride by holding on to what I thought was right in my eyes. I told her I forgave her, but my actions said something different. My words did not align with my actions. I remember many times walking by her in the hallway at work and the silence was loud and uncomfortable. Our spirits were battling. No one was winning. Flesh was on parade. It is a fact that we feel emotions, but our behaviors can be controlled.

CHAPTER THIRTEEN - STILL WATERS

## Layers on Layers

I was building a case as if I had a jury on my side that was going to help me settle my truth. The hurt I felt cut a part of me that was supposed to remain whole. I am sure you can identify those times in your life when you experienced hurt, and those old wounds wanted to burst back open. Toxic. Poisonous. Layers on layers of cuts and bruises can be damaging to your future. This disappointment felt deeper than a surface cut. It went past the fascia–the thin layer that covers the body from becoming exposed to the outside.

The love of God holds our minds and emotions in place, not allowing the pain of yesterday to mingle with our new days. The love of God is our fascia. God's love shields us from diseases and foreign objects. But here we go again, back down memory lane. Our minds are programmed to dig up and redo all the old junk. It is a tricky pattern of the Enemy–a classic.

Hurt will cause you to look different on the inside. What have hurt, offense, and disappointments caused you to look like? Are you unloving, cold, bitter, unsympathetic, judgmental, mean, egotistical, selfish... Check your heart. Expose every disappointment. It is necessary so you can feel better. Why keep it to yourself and continue to live in a tender place? Think about it.

The Lord soon visited me. He said, "Well, Vicki, did disappointment cause you to forget the God you serve?" I then thought if God allowed this situation in my life, there is something He wants me to learn. Honesty comes in different forms at different angles. I, too, was dishonest. It all became a game, and the Enemy was still winning. I allowed him to win. I learned we can speak through our lips, but our hearts are far from the truth when we allow disappointment to become a matter of the heart. Be reminded:

> The heart is deceitful above all things, and desperately wicked: who can know it? I the LORD search the heart, I try the reins, even to give every man according to

his ways, and according to the fruit of his doings.
(Jeremiah 17:9-10)

A new heart also will I give you, and a new spirit will I put within you: and I will take away the stony heart out of your flesh, and I will give you a heart of flesh.
(Ezekiel 36:26)

## Don't Hold People Hostage

I remember sitting at my desk at work, and the Holy Spirit spoke to me, "Don't hold people hostage; release her."

Immediately, I said, "What, Lord? How?"

The Lord ministered to me, "You keep people hostage when you keep their faults before them, causing them to relive their wrong. I am God, and I don't need your help judging those you think are wrong."

Ouch! I immediately felt His conviction. I was so convicted. I began to weep, and I instantly ran to tell her, "I forgive you and please forgive me." You may be saying, "Why did you ask her to forgive you?" Because although she betrayed my trust, my actions were wrong. The Lord also allowed me to minister to her. She never once apologized but at this point, it was okay. I was responsible for my actions and shortcomings.

*We are judged by the way we respond.*

When we get to heaven and stand before God, He will not ask us what someone did to us. We are judged by the way we respond. I pray that God would give her the grace to do just as I did. I thank God for His grace to release and

## CHAPTER THIRTEEN – STILL WATERS

move on. I thank God that His grace gave me the strength and ability to see past my own selfish emotions. Many times, we want God to give us grace, but we dare not give grace to others.

I am sure you have experienced a time when you felt your heart was ripped right out of your chest. Disappointments have a way of making you stop and immediately throw you into panic attacks. This is a clever design of the Enemy. What is the one threat against the Enemy when faced with disappointments?

## Prayer Is the Antidote

Do you know prayer is the force that makes everything okay? Prayer is your weapon against all that tries to defeat you. Prayer unlocks every area in your heart and mind that disappointments have taken residence in. Prayer is the antidote that counteracts the cycle of disappointments. Disappointments will take you in cycles–painful chaotic cycles. You have given the disappointments too much of your energy. That was the plan of the Enemy in the first place.

What are the disappointments many face today that have caused them to be stuck?

- ♥ Death
- ♥ Illness and disease
- ♥ Rape
- ♥ Molestation
- ♥ Lies
- ♥ Abandonment
- ♥ Divorce
- ♥ Adultery
- ♥ Hate crimes
- ♥ Loss of jobs
- ♥ Rejection

- ♥ Loss of relationships
- ♥ Failure
- ♥ Mistreatment

Life happens. Let us admit some happenings do not feel good, but there is something about prayer. Prayer will heal each broken part of you. Prayer will touch parts of you that call for change. Prayer settles you in a still place. (Take a deep breath here.)

Some of us are disappointed with God. Why? At times, we cannot understand His ways and decisions. We long for understanding and some closure. We feel God has not answered, healed, or helped us. Achieving the promise is a long journey and the pain seems eternal. I have learned in times of uncertainty to trust in the promise rather than the process. The promises of God are sure and amen. The process can change at a moment's notice, but the promise is the Word of God, and it remains true. When filled with disappointments, you must ask God to help your faith factor.

You can run to the Father and be even more vulnerable, releasing every thought to Him. His grace is there as your divine intervention. God will disrupt some things for your peace. His grace is the ally in disappointments. His stillness is sweet. His stillness overshadows your hurt and warms your soul with gladness.

## Still Waters

Have you ever sat by a lake and listened to the sound of calmness? You sit there, close your eyes and meditate on the goodness of the Father. It is so peaceful and surreal. It stops you from panicking and gives you peace. Allow your mind to transition to that peaceful place. I can recall a time sitting in my back yard looking into my swimming pool; the water was still. The wind was blowing; the trees were singing; birds were chirping, but the water was still. That is just like God. When we are in a state of panic and decide to trust Him… there is stillness.

## CHAPTER THIRTEEN – STILL WATERS

In that stillness, we learn that our most challenging disappointments also become our greatest encouragement because of the Word.

> He leads me beside still waters; he restoreth my soul.
> (Psalm 23:2b)

It is supernatural peace. God has heard your prayer requests. No matter what you are going through, nothing compares to God's stillness. God's presence shows up in stillness. His stillness will turn your chaotic situation into a picture of peace. You must trust God to do that for you. Trust God to be everything you need Him to be. The Word declares, "He leads me beside the still waters." And the Word did not stop there. It proceeds to say, "He restoreth my soul." God leads us to stillness.

*Trust in the promise rather than the process.*

He restores us and mends all the broken pieces. We are restored to freedom, and everything out of order in our lives is put in place. Your test of disappointment is now your testimony. A huge mess is now a message to others that God takes rambunctious, raging water and makes it still. In quietness, we search for the parts of us that need restoring. Look at your heart; does it need mending? God restores. God is 100% capable of restoring you to complete wholeness. God invests in situations that seem impossible.

## Chapter 14

# Relentless

The Enemy is relentless and will not stop being a negative force. We live in a time when believers are yielding and surrendering their weapons to him. What weapons? The weapons of prayer and praise. These have become dormant simply because believers' faith has been pressed by worry, fear, and anxiety.

The Enemy has entered their spaces without permission or notice and forced himself into their lives. He is not renting space; he is living there for free. In other words, the Enemy is allowed to govern, and there is no fight to kick him out. The Enemy watches our lives extensively and studies us. He will violate our spaces. It is the worse feeling in the world to be violated! But why are we surprised when we have dropped our guard and placed our weapons on the shelf?

It is called being comfortable. Do not get comfortable flirting with the Enemy. You have come too far to become comfortable. It is dangerous. The Enemy is cunning and will show up without a moment's notice. He will challenge you on so many levels. He shows up like a big, old bully buffeting the people of God with trickery and antagonizing them with manipulation. The Enemy shows up in different forms and using different strategies. The Enemy diligently targets the minds of people with pictures of pleasure causing them to lose focus on what is real and meaningful in their lives.

I have learned the Enemy is super smart at making people feel it is okay to remain defeated and oppressed. It is not okay. The Enemy knows if you stay in that space, you will revert to self-destructive behaviors: suicidal thoughts, drugs, and alcohol. The Enemy targets people with illusions making them feel the need to be something different than what God has created them to be. For example, 2 Corinthians 11:14 warns us, "And no wonder, for Satan disguises him as an angel of light." Satan deceives us by appearing as light, something good. His goal is to break you down and reduce you to nothing. He wants to take you into a deep place of innate darkness by isolation. Then he robs you of your self-worth and self-esteem. He is relentless. You cannot allow his schemes to work. You must know the Enemy's resume to defeat him; it is found in the Word of God. We apply the Word of God to the strategies of the Enemy to defeat him. The Enemy has three points on his agenda.

1. **Steal**
2. **Kill**
3. **Destroy**

> The thief cometh not, but for to steal, and to kill, and to destroy: I am come that they might have life, and that they might have it more abundantly. (John 10:10-11)

This is the Enemy's agenda, which will never change. He is relentless and does not play fair. The Word of God describes him as a thief. He plays for keeps and has no sympathy. Do not give him permission to take anything in your life. Do not get comfortable in your prayer life. Be constant in prayer daily. Allow prayer to be your daily communion with the Father.

Prayer is our weapon; we use it to fight and win. We are in warfare fighting many battles against the Enemy daily to survive naturally and spiritually. From my personal experiences, I have learned that sometimes, in our moments of rest, in our times of contentment, when all seems well, the Enemy attempts to hurt us the most. Be reminded by this scripture:

CHAPTER FOURTEEN - RELENTLESS

> Be sober-minded, be watchful. Your adversary the devil prowls around like a roaring lion, seeking someone to devour. (1 Peter 5:8)

The Enemy makes things appear greater than what they are. He creates deception in our eyes and thoughts. For example, he makes a lie look like the truth. He makes suggestions that cause us to act on untruths rooted in deception.

## Eve Was Deceived

I recall the story of Eve in Genesis Chapter 3. I encourage you to read the passage of Scripture and learn. Eve was deceived. She had everything, but Satan tricked her into eating the forbidden fruit. Lies! Relentless! Do not be deceived by the hype. Eve believed the hype of this deceiving, cunning liar. Here is the truth then the lie, which contradicted God's Word.

> Now the serpent was more subtle than any beast of the field which the Lord God had made. And he said unto the woman, Yea, hath God said, Ye shall not eat of every tree of the garden? And the woman said unto the serpent, We may eat of the fruit of the trees of the garden: But of the fruit of the tree which is in the midst of the garden, God hath said, Ye shall not eat of it, neither shall ye touch it, lest ye die. And the serpent said unto the woman, Ye shall not surely die: For God doth know that in the day ye eat thereof, then your eyes shall be opened, and ye shall be as gods, knowing good and evil. (Genesis 3:1-5)

Eve knew God but was tricked because she listened to Satan talk too long and became weak. The Enemy was subtle, and he confused Eve's mind. Do not water Satan's lies or entertain them by rehashing them in your mind, talking about them with others, or even conversing with him as Eve did. When you feed the lie it will grow. When it grows, it becomes a stronghold in your life because you have made it larger than God.

## Ultimate Agenda

John 10:10 speaks of the thief: one who takes without permission. The thief is slick and sly. He creeps into our lives secretly to take what is rightfully ours. The thief carefully and purposefully maps out his plot and then he makes his hit. He steals our possessions and puts them to wrong use.

Eve was pure and special, but the Enemy took advantage of her by stealing her purity causing her to question Who God is. Eve was made to feel as if she was missing out on something better. The Enemy worked hard and succeeded at sabotaging God's Word in her life. Peace and harmony were stolen from her.

Satan was one of the prettiest angels in heaven; however, he thought he was above God. From the very beginning, Satan, the Enemy, has been trying to separate mankind and eliminate them through sin. The very reason Satan was kicked out of heaven was because of his deceitful nature, which he used to try to take God's throne. Satan makes everything about himself; he is full of pride.

The thief is like a hunter. He and all his friends are attempting to destroy everything good in your life. It is his pleasure to rob you of everything you have worked hard for. Remember taking is his ultimate agenda. The thief dives deeper by robbing us of peace, joy, happiness, our families, minds, passion, characters, smiles, and the list continues. He destroys all that is fruitful if allowed. While studying John 10:10, I read an article that describes the thief's mission and nature. Pay close attention.

> *The word "thief" comes from the Greek word klepto, which means to steal. It gives a picture of a bandit, pickpocket, or thief who is so artful in the way he steals that his exploits of thievery are nearly*

## CHAPTER FOURTEEN – RELENTLESS

> *undetectable. This reminds me of the pickpockets who work the streets in certain areas of Moscow. They can slip their hands into a person's pockets, take what they want, and be long gone before that person discovers they were even there! Jesus uses this word to let us know the devil is very cunning in the way he steals from people. He knows that if he does it outright, his actions will be recognized; therefore, he steals from people in such a deceptive way that he often accomplishes his evil goal before they even know he has stolen from them! Often the devil injects thoughts into a person's mind to steal his peace, his joy, and even his beliefs. The word* klepto *describes a thief's uncontrollable urge to get his hands into someone's pockets so he can take that which does not rightfully belong to him. I find it remarkably interesting that this is where we get the word kleptomaniac, which describes a person with a persistent, neurotic impulse to steal. Just as a kleptomaniac can't help but steal, the devil can't stop stealing because it is his impulse and his very nature to steal. This is precisely the nature and behavior of the thief Jesus told us about!*[ix]

Sly!

Dirty!

Smart!

Strategic!

Clever!

Cunning!

What has the Enemy stolen from you? _____ .

Be thoughtful. Listen to your heart and answer honestly.

Be watchful! Be alert! Do not be tricked or robbed by the Enemy. Remember the thief comes to do all these things; however, the Lord said, "I am come that they might have life and that they might have it more abundantly" (John 10:10). That is grace.

In times when the Enemy's attempt is strongest, grace is present. We know what the Enemy is capable of. We recognize the authority he has, but what about our God? He is greater. 1 John 4:4 decrees that greater is He that is in me than He that is in the world. God has all power. He is limitless, and we have access to that power. We are not less than or equal to the Enemy, but we are greater. Aren't you glad you know God? There are true benefits to having a relationship with God.

## Uncertain in a Safe Place

The worse feeling in the world is when you have been robbed. Unfortunately, many people have experienced times in their lives when the Enemy has forced them into mental and physical obscurity to take advantage of them. I remember a painful story of a young girl. The Enemy robbed her of her innocence through assault, abuse, and molestation (ugly words).

As young girls, we look to older males and females in our lives for protection and direction. Young girls are taught that older boys are their protection. What happens in the mind of a young girl when the person who is supposed to protect her becomes the predator? The Enemy uses people who will allow him to hurt people! What happens when the protector takes advantage of her? Beware! The Enemy presents himself in different forms. He appears as a flattering friend or family member.

In the blink of an eye, this young girl became subject to the trauma designed by the Enemy. Without notice, the Enemy began to take precedence in a place initially designed for her safety. She was confused, betrayed, and scared to speak. Her story crushes me! Does this sound familiar to anyone? There is no doubt it does.

This young girl who was full of light became uncertain in her safe place. She was not sure how to comprehend the situation at such a

## CHAPTER FOURTEEN - RELENTLESS

young age. This relative who was once identified as a protector no longer held that role in her life. She was only six or seven years old. Look how smooth the Enemy presented betrayal. She lost her sense of safety because the very person who was supposed to protect her took advantage of her trust in him. Sadly, she had no clue how to truly feel. She was young and innocent. The tactic of an enemy is to set you up and make you feel helpless, guilty, and confused at the same time. It is difficult to see beyond the mixture of emotions. Once emotions have set in and are bottled up, they become your friend.

> *We do not seek revenge against the offender; instead, we forgive.*

Silence is another weapon the Enemy uses to keep you in darkness. The Enemy is a master planner. Think about what this little girl experienced. Just imagine. She was afraid to tell anyone because she worried no one would believe her at the tender age of six. This is the truth, and it is real for many girls and boys. Her mind took the responsibility for the incident and she thought she would get in trouble for what was happening. She was trapped in her thoughts which were filled with questions.

The Enemy plays emotional mind games that appear real to the victim. Her words were, "I thought it was my fault." How dare the Enemy create pain in her life then take that same pain and use it against her! Again, beware of his weapon of self-sabotage. He will create pain in your life and fight you until he has conquered you. Don't allow him to win. He is a thief, but grace covers. Grace will give you the wherewithal to stand when you want to crumble. Grace from God alone will give you the mental energy to defeat him. Grace will give you the tenacity to save you. Grace will help you walk through the shame.

## Ultimate Protection

The Enemy attempted to kill her confidence, destroy her sense of safety and security, and take her voice. He even sought to alter her view of men and open the door to other destructive avenues–beginning at the early age of six. But look at the power of God. As she matured, she began to understand John 10:10b, "I come that they might have life and that they might have it more abundantly." She came to understand that Christ offered the ultimate protection! The Enemy's plan to plant seeds of low self-esteem, promiscuity, resentment, hostility, anger, and victimization failed. This life sentence of darkness would not be her testimony. Grace protected her from continuing the cycle and becoming the abuser. Do you understand what I just said? She could have in turn become the offender. She declared she would not repeat the offense. That's grace.

If you see yourself in this story, you are not alone. There are many children and youth who have been violated. The lie is victims will never recover or heal. The truth is God's grace is sufficient and available. Grace is the sweet presence that makes it all better.

Therapy by a trained and experienced professional will help an individual process and move forward in life and heal. It is necessary. Sexual abuse is not just a physical action. It includes the invasion of the mind. It is mental. It is emotional.

For some, it is hard to reconcile the why. Why did this happen to me? They realize years later it was wrong. On the other hand, for others, it is all about getting revenge. I will make them pay for what they did! The thought of your virtue being violated makes you angry. You crave for the perpetrator to suffer as you suffered! Pain and frustration can be explosive. And I get it! You want to make the offender hurt. Bad! Real Bad! The Enemy will steal, kill and, in turn, take your anger and make you harm the offender. However, the Word of God encourages us not to take revenge but leave room for God's wrath. For it is written:

> It is mine to avenge; I will repay, says the LORD.
> (Romans 12:19, NIV)

By God's grace, we do not seek revenge against the offender; instead, we forgive. Lord teach us how to forgive in situations like this. For some, forgiveness is a long work in process. The desire to take revenge consumes our thoughts and forces us to adopt destructive mindsets of one day hurting the offender. If this is how you feel, instead of destroying yourself with this mindset, pray. I often say keep your mouth moving, keep talking to God. Ask God to teach you how to forgive and to deliver the person from his or her demonic thoughts, so they will not hurt anyone else. Admittedly, this is not easy, it can be a challenging and painful process, but it is crucial to your well-being.

## Change the Trajectory

We must seek revenge against Satan, our Enemy, the strategist behind all the pain. We get revenge against him by restructuring our stories. We change the trajectory by encouraging every girl or boy, man or woman who has ever been taken advantage of sexually, physically and emotionally to speak up. Tell and expose!

Don't let the Enemy steal your voice. We get revenge by doing as the Word of God tells us in Jude 23a: "Save others by snatching them from the fire." Grace snatches us out of the fire.

Keeping Satan's secrets makes us accomplices to his crimes and the victims of the tragic stories he authors. Pray. Tell Jesus. Make an arrest in the spirit realm. Uncover it! Set yourself free. Don't stay silent. Naively, by staying silent, we are guilty of aiding and abetting and are now accessories to the crimes committed against us. Now is the time to stop protecting the predators who stole our strength to speak. We must start exposing them! Prayer will give you wisdom and timing.

We command the Enemy to drop his weapons.

God's grace will take the sting of pain and resentment and refresh you to live the greater life He promised. He promised us lives of abundance, wholeness, peace, prosperity, joy, opportunity, healing, and favor. I invite you to be a partaker in this life of abundance. Look at what happened when you were violated. Some of the items the Enemy stole you may never retrieve. That is a harsh reality, but the great news is God will bless you with more. God will even bless you with better. The truth is you may never get over it, but grace will get you through it.

> Now thanks be unto God, which always causeth us to triumph in Christ. (2 Corinthians 2:14)

Be aware of the Enemy's truths.

The Devil wants you to be defeated.

The Devil wants you to struggle through your entire life.

The Devil wants you to be sick, depressed, down in the dumps, glum, and miserable.

The Devil wants you to feel like you will never hit the target with your life.

> *Jesus wants to give you a life that is unrivaled, unequaled, matchless, incomparable, richly loaded, and overflowing with life to the ultimate maximum!*[xi]

The Enemy is a relentless thief but thank God for His grace. Thank you, Maxine (now a licensed Evangelist), for allowing me to tell your story. You are more than a conqueror. Remarkably, your pain is a testimony of God's grace. You are more than an overcomer. Someone will be delivered, healed and exposed by your testimony.

# Chapter 15

# Grace Wins

God, your grace is my peace and calmness when I feel like quitting. Seriously! Grace is my calmness when my will feels as if it has come to an end, when I am tired. Can you relate? I am sure you can. You tried faithfully to remain in that sacred place, but situations come to test you, not once, but repeatedly–distractions. At this point, I often found myself rationalizing my feelings and thoughts just to make it through the day. I thought I could not tell anyone because I assumed they would not understand. Would they utterly understand? Would they have the patience to sympathize, listen, care, not judge or run and tell? Let's admit–some things are just too juicy to keep to ourselves. I would laugh often and say, "Someone must be anointed to keep my secrets!" When all is said and done, I often settle in knowing that remaining quiet is the best and most suitable option for me.

Learning the art of silence is priceless, but the buildup is a volcano just waiting to explode in your mind. A meltdown can pop up out of nowhere, but thankfully, that voice of grace kicks in softly and boldly. It speaks to your inner man to remind you not to adhere to the inner enemy. You will continue to fight. The inner enemy is your thoughts; it's you. We fight against ourselves. It's not always other people. In our minds, we work hard to figure out what is going on with us. It is an inner battle, but grace wins the very moment we allow God to do His work within us.

Have you ever been in a fight of your life trying to stay afloat? Have you ever been swallowed up by the crashing waves of the ocean at high tide? You tried to escape but it came so quickly the sand moved beneath your feet and the water pulled you deeper. The ocean waters often win. They are strong. Symbolically, life will pull you under if you don't fight to stay above the high tide. Mental toughness, confidence, and prayer sustain you.

While writing this chapter, my mind traveled back to when my daughter, Alexandria, was in the 10th grade, her sophomore year of high school. She was a devout basketball player and incredibly dedicated to the game. She absolutely loved it; so much so, she would sleep with her basketball if her dad or I let her. From an incredibly young age, it was her dream to be a ballplayer and to one day earn a basketball scholarship. She wanted to become a Division One athlete. Alex had natural talent and ability, and she had the brains. She was indeed confident in the skills and gifts God gave her.

One summer, I picked her up from a basketball camp hosted at UC Santa Barbara. She was tired but very excited. That same weekend, she had a basketball tournament in Bakersfield at the local university, CSUB. Her dad was out of town and we spoke to him by telephone on the ride home. He suggested she rest and not play in the game, but Alex insisted. Fast forward to the game. Alex was going up for a shot when her opponent fell on her. The crowd roared because you could hear the impact of them falling to the ground. I did not see Alex get up from the floor. I only saw her grabbing her knee. When I saw her face, I could tell she was in terrible pain. As I got closer, I saw why. Her coach picked her up and rushed her to my car so I could transport her to the emergency room. My youngest daughter, Alexis, her baby sister, had such love and concern, she began crying. With tears falling from her face, she repeatedly asked, "Mom, is sissy okay?"

Alex was examined and sent home. We were told to keep her leg iced, to have her take Motrin every six hours as needed for pain, and to follow-up with an orthopedic doctor because her knee was too swollen to take an X-ray. Talk about worrying! Thank you Lord for my village

CHAPTER FIFTEEN - GRACE WINS

of sisters that stayed the night ensuring that we were ok. Doubt and fear crept in so easily as if they were my best friends. We all knew Alex's passion for the game. All we could think about was if she would be able to play again. She had just received word the week before that she'd been selected as a potential scholarship candidate at the prestigious New Hampshire-based university, Dartmouth College. We just knew there was no way her dreams would be shattered. We had faith.

Alex was finally able to get an appointment with an orthopedic doctor. Of course, I was there. Her knee was examined, and an MRI was ordered. We waited patiently in faith, laughing together to ease the anxiety that tried so hard to settle in our hearts and minds.

The doctor returned to the room, and I will never forget the words he said, "Alexandria, I'm sorry to tell you this; you have torn your ACL, MCL, and meniscus, and your basketball career is over." What! You are kidding me! I responded before my mind could even process the doctor's diagnosis, "Oh, we don't receive that." The look of sadness in her eyes was distressing. My heart began to race. Alexandria grabbed her face and began to cry. Humbly, she said with a low voice, "Oh, no, are you sure?"

He said, "Yes, I'm so sorry."

What do you mean she's done? She is just a tenth grader! I could not conceptualize the loss of the dream my daughter held for so long. He replied, "Okay, well, I'll tell you what. We will get you into surgery; repair your injury; order you to have extensive physical therapy for one whole year, and you *may* be able to return to basketball to play your senior year." I could see that Alex felt a little bit better after he expressed his concerns and suggestions, but the disappointment did not go away.

After a few weeks, she went into surgery. The entire process was a huge learning experience. She suffered in pain and learned a lot about life during this time of healing. As varsity captain, she faithfully served her basketball team by showing up to practice daily and attended all the games. Although she could not play, she supported them and was their best cheerleader. Alex returned to school on crutches. She earned good grades. She was indeed a champion. How in the world could a young lady, only in the 10th grade, experience such loss yet show up to be her best self? It was because of grace. God's grace allowed her to play her senior year.

Let me give you a golden nugget here. You may feel as if you have been knocked out of the game of life. Nevertheless, you must focus on our Father's prescription. Alex focused on the prescription her doctor gave her, and she had faith in God's promise. God's grace always wins.

## Key Points to Letting Grace Win

- ♥ Listen
- ♥ Stay focused
- ♥ Do not complain
- ♥ Do not allow disappointment to knock you out of the game of life
- ♥ Follow what the Father has prescribed for you
- ♥ Show up for your assignment
- ♥ Be consistent despite your ailment

## CHAPTER FIFTEEN – GRACE WINS

- ♥ Be mentally tough
- ♥ Don't give up because of a negative report
- ♥ Although broken, declare yourself healed

Senior year! Through depression, loss, anxiety, sadness, and therapy, she was back on the court in her senior year of high school. Not only was she back on the court, but she also helped her team make it to the Valley Championship game in Fresno, California. Not only did she make it to the Valley championship game, but she also helped her team *win* by shooting two three-pointers back-to-back, putting the team back in the game after they'd been down several points.

I will never forget when they won the championship. Her teammates ran to her, embraced her, and loved on her because they knew what she went through with her knee. Grace wins every time. God is so merciful. He shows up in the small things in our lives and turns them into overabundant, miraculous testimonies of victory.

Fast forward. Alex graduated from high school and attends California State University, Fullerton, but the residue of loss followed her. She longed to play basketball. However, that inner voice was a constant reminder her injury would not allow her to do so as a Division One athlete. Although she loved basketball, she did not pursue playing in college. I remember the day she called her father and said, "Dad, I couldn't even walk in the gym." She was weeping on the phone. As parents, we prayed; we listened; we let her talk, but we knew she would have to figure this out within her spirit and come to a resolution. As time went by, she became better, but we knew the remnants of hurt and disappointment were still present.

One day, we got a call from Alex. She told us she was sitting in the cafeteria and a gentleman approached her. He said, "Young lady, you look pretty strong. Have you ever thought about going out for track and field?"

Alex said she chuckled, "What? I'm too big to be trying to be on the track team."

He said, "Have you ever thought about coming out to throw the weighted ball or the hammer?"

She responded, "I guess I'll try. What harm would it be?"

Alex was placed on a two-week trial to see if she was good enough to make the team. But after just three days, the coach said to her, "You are incredible; how about you join us."

To this day, we laugh about this experience. Where the grace of God follows you, grace will win every time. Grace recompensed our daughter for all she lost while in high school. Alex had a prayer to be a Division One athlete. Grace did that for her. Grace afforded her the opportunity to travel first class on airplanes, athletic buses and participate from state to state, city to city in track and field as a Division One athlete and placing 8th in the Big West Conference, placing 4th at the Cal/Nevada Championship and her best was placing 2nd at Northern Arizona Team Challenge in the hammer throw. This was a huge accomplishment. God restores and gives us double after our losses. Be encouraged by this:

> I will restore the years that the locust has eaten.
> (Joel 2:25)
>
> *Money can be restored. Property can be restored—broken-down cars, stripped painting, old houses. Relationships can be restored. But one thing that can never be restored is time. Time flies and it does not return. Years pass and we never get them back.*[xii]

God said He will restore the years you have lost and will still give you a testimony. God will turn your pain and misery into something glorious. It will be a blessing and testimony to others looking on. Grace allows you to stay focused with passion. Don't complain, friends. Look to God for all things and declare that God, *our God*, is your source. He will give you the desires of your heart.

Why did I call this chapter "Grace Wins"? Because grace had the final say in my daughter's situation. Whatever you are going through right now in your life, know God will take every burden and turn it into a blessing. He will take every stumbling block and turn it into a steppingstone. He makes peace for time lost. Believe this.

> And we know that in all things God works for the good of those who love him, who have been called according to his purpose. (Romans 8:28)

Grace is a part of His "all things." Grace is that incessant voice, which shouts loudly and cheers you on when life has given you a beating. Grace is that steady hand when your passion is challenged. Grace is that stillness when the Enemy wants to taunt you about what appears to be lost. With assurance, you must believe in the God of the Bible. No matter what it looks like or what the Enemy wraps it up with to make us feel hopeless, grace abounds. We serve and trust a true and living God who will perform according to His will and purpose. In the preceding scripture, it declares that all things are working for our good, whether ugly, unjust, or unfair. Problems may come to cripple us and distort our view of our purpose in life, but God works it all out.

## We Will Fix It

Another touchy moment I remember all too well is when my youngest daughter, Alexis, fell ill. I was at work and my husband called saying she had fallen from the bed and seemed lethargic. She wasn't talking as much as she had been earlier in the day. Mind you, she was an active 18-month-old toddler, so quiet was not her thing. He took her to the emergency room, and I met him there. She was examined over and over; we were there the entire day and no doctor could tell us what was wrong with her. Our faith was challenged. We knew something was just not right, but what do you do when everything and everyone around you says something different?

An ER specialty physician came to our room. Her name was Dr. Kumari. I will never forget her. She was an angel. She touched Alexis' stomach, turned to my husband and me, and said, "Here's the problem; her bowels are blocked." She was right. Alexis was diagnosed with intussusception of the bowels; there was 80% blockage. Our baby girl was sick and needed surgery! No surgeon in Kern County would agree to operate on her bowels because she was so young, and her organs were fragile. They feared her bowels would rupture. Grace was working all the while. She was immediately transferred to UCLA Medical Center by ambulance. I rode with her; only one of us could. I will never forget my husband's face as we drove off. He was so worried about his baby girl. I could see it in his eyes.

We cried and we prayed. We stood in faith that the Devil would not steal our seed and the God of all grace would cover her. Alexis was a strong baby. I'm sure this is why she's so confident, strong, and determined today.

When we arrived at UCLA hospital, the surgeons met us at the door and their words were, "Welcome to UCLA Hospital. We will fix it." God guided their hands and blessed us even more. Alexis did not need surgery after all. The medical team was quick to correct the issue with a less invasive procedure. Alexis was back to her playful self after the procedure. Our baby girl was healed. The Enemy tried it–but God! Once again, our faith was challenged but grace always wins.

God takes the most complicated, intricate, impossible situations and molds them in His hands to do as He pleases. If you are ever in doubt when you are up against a problem that seems insurmountable, know that all things are working together for your good. The word "working" lets us know God is fighting. He is doing the tough work for your good. Shout out loud and say, "I declare it's working for my good!" Say it fearlessly and without hesitation. It is working!

## Chapter 16

# Sea Sickness

Have you ever been on a boat or a ship? What about taking a boat ride on rough waters? The waves toss back and forth rhythmically. Not being used to the rhythm, you begin to feel lightheaded, dizzy, and a little nauseous. Suddenly, you are bent over in pain. You are seasick. The urgency to get back to shore is unlike anything you have experienced before. Fast or slow, smooth, or rough, the ride is still unbearable, and you are still sick.

Here is my first experience with seasickness. My family and I were on a quick ride for the day. The ride was only an hour-and-a-half long but required a short boat ride to reach the small, romantic island we had planned to visit. I felt queasy almost immediately. I said to myself, "I want to get off this boat." The rigid ups and downs of the waves and the rocking left to right caused much havoc in my tummy!

No one told me to take medication or to prepare for the likelihood of seasickness. I was incredibly frustrated and mad. Interestingly, I found it convenient to blame others for my unpreparedness. We finally made it to Catalina Island. She was beautiful–but more of a beautiful disaster for me. I spent the entire day on land vomiting. It was horrible.

While everyone was having a great time, I was balled up on a bench, miserable, begging my husband to find a helicopter to get me back to my car. I tried and tried, but it wasn't happening. We had come too far. I had to–I needed to–stick it out. And when I did, I got relief. But the relief was a long process. Thank God for grace!

The waiting game can be a hard pill to swallow, but for me, the wait was exactly what I needed. Think back to a time when you had to wait for something to work itself out. Can you see it? I had to wait for my healing and deliverance from seasickness. The little white Dramamine pill wasn't doing the job. It just simply wasn't enough. Time was my solution. And I had to wait for it.

## The Ride Back Home

The thought of getting back on that boat made me even sicker. I was mad at myself for not researching what a first-time boat ride might be like. It is fair to say I was a bit too comfortable. Catalina Island taught me a lesson I will never forget–be prepared. I'm grateful for the grace of God that got me through the day.

There are times when we make mistakes because we are not prepared, and we get too comfortable. We dive into situations that catch us off guard and make us sick. The process of coming out of our tests can be cumbersome and confusing. If we are truly honest, sometimes we bring these circumstances on ourselves. If we are confused, God is our absolute best point of reference.

If you seek Him, He will not allow you to be seasick, confused, and overcome by the tides and waves in your life. He is the source of calmness. He shapes our outcomes and knows the paths we must take to get to our destinations. Healthy prayer lives (meaning talking to God often, daily) and true relationships with God are the best preparation for the unexpected rifts in our future. Prayer is a posture. We may not have all the right words, but God honors the words from our hearts. There is no perfect prayer but there is the perfect truth.

Sometimes we get seasick because we take situations into our own hands. We fail to talk to God about them. We look for solutions without resting in God's purpose and timing. I believe God is smiling and saying to us: "I get it. I understand. I feel you, but I did not ask you to take problems upon yourself. I did not ask you to let issues build up residue in your mind. I did not ask you to carry them to the point you became emotionally sick. I asked you to cast every care you have on Me. I asked you to give it to Me because I am God."

When we function in our own understanding, rather than consulting the Father, we become sick. It is a fact. For years many of us have been walking, processing, and maneuvering in that same pattern–consulting self. But I encourage you when you are confused or emotionally sick, trust God.

> *We look for solutions without resting in God's purpose and timing.*

When your spiritual equilibrium is off, God is your remedy. If you seek Him, He will bring balance to your life. When we fail to consult God, our minds, emotions, and zeal are shaped by our processes. Remember this important fact, we must allow God to peel away the layers of distrust in Him and reveal to us a better way of living. Our way of living must rest in God's will. It is the grace of God that has granted us the favor to keep going. We will not crash. We will not be cast onto the shore. We will not remain sick. We will survive and be well.

Thank God for grace.

CHAPTER 17

# DEEP WATERS

> Then they cried to the Lord in their trouble, and he delivered them from their distress. He made the storm be still, and the waves of the sea were hushed. Then they were glad that the waters were quiet, and he brought them to their desired haven. (Psalm 107:28-30)

"And the waves and the seas were hushed." Ah, that's good news. That is our reassurance. Peace is our portion. Deep waters are symbolic of all the adversities we experience. Deep waters! Trouble. Danger. Chaos. Uncertainty. I hope you will comprehend how God adores you. The love of God is all around you, and the way He envisions you is remarkable. If you are facing adversity, I pray you will know God's peace and grace when you put your faith in Him.

We will experience life on many levels, and we will be challenged to the point of drowning. But God assures us through His nature that He is with us even in stormy weather. Have you ever experienced a storm? Flashing lightning, thick darkness, roaring thunder, and the whistling winds shake all the windows causing you to fear. It is overwhelming. In the storm, you must grip faith and silence the destructive thoughts. Cleave to our Father Who is the Author and the Finisher of our faith.

"The waters were quiet." Soothing. Calming. Refreshing. Gentle. The deepest parts of your life that were loud and full of discomfort are now quiet. The parts of you that succumbed to your emotions and were all bottled up are now released. Take a deep breath. Now, release.

The truth is all of your adversities may never go away. However, in the midst of them, you can experience peace and quietness. The grace of God will seep through giving you the wherewithal to stand firm. When we are reminded of God's presence, it assures us that trouble won't last always. I remember singing a song in the choir, "I'm so glad trouble doesn't last always." What a relief it is to know that. It inspires faith. God may decide to eradicate our troubles or choose to stretch us through them causing discomfort. This may be a way to bring maturity or prepare us for better. We must believe we have everything we need because His grace abounds. Thank You, Jesus. I screamed out loud right here.

*God will push you above the deep waters that hold you down.*

When struggling in deep waters, it is comforting to feel that sudden peace grip you like a cloak reassuring you God loves you. That love trumps all the emotions which have been bottled up inside for so many reasons causing us to sink. God will see you through. God will push you above the deep waters of life that hold you down. These deep waters of distress make you say, "I'm sinking. I can't go any further! I'm done. I'm done trying to compete with what we call life."

Why are you competing with life? God did not design you to do that. We must see winning through the eyes of faith. Watch your words for they determine the courses of your life. I heard someone say, "You must push through the deep waters that intimidate you." We tend to lose control because of what we see or hear that causes our feelings to get the best of us. Now you know that sometimes our emotions tend to get the best of us. Listen, silence those emotions. When plunging in deep waters, be reminded of the Gospel of Mark when God rebuked the storm:

> And he arose, and rebuked the wind, and said unto the sea, Peace, be still. And the wind ceased, and there was a great calm. (Mark 4:39)

Jesus arose and rebuked the wind. He spoke directly to the sea and it became still. During your greatest challenges and most demanding moments, the Enemy will create his top-secret concoctions. But God is your calmness. Remember the authority God has given you on the earth; use it. Declare it. My lifeline to you is this:

- ♥ Be strong
- ♥ Be vigilant
- ♥ Trust God
- ♥ Takes lots of deep breaths
- ♥ Inhale and exhale
- ♥ Pat yourself on the back
- ♥ Be patient with you
- ♥ Give yourself some grace (Thank you, Camille)
- ♥ Never compromise
- ♥ Your weakness is your strength
- ♥ Love each day with all of your being
- ♥ Appreciate grace
- ♥ Don't allow life to make you drown
- ♥ Remember that each day is a gift–tough or easy
- ♥ Forgive and live
- ♥ Face your pain and keep swimming until you learn

- ♥ Talk to God every day; when you can't find the words, whisper something
- ♥ It is never too late to take swimming lessons

Remember this:

> When thou passest through the waters, I will be with thee; and through the rivers, they shall not overflow thee. (Isaiah 43:2)

## Conclusion

This book would not be complete if I did not offer you the plan of salvation. Salvation in itself is grace.

> That if you confess with your mouth the Lord Jesus and believe in your heart that God has raised Him from the dead, you will be saved. For with the heart one believes unto righteousness, and with the mouth confession is made unto salvation.
> (Romans 10:9-10, NKJV)

God gave His Son Jesus Christ so you could experience a relationship with Him like no other. If you would like to have a personal encounter with God's grace, pray this prayer from your heart out loud:

> *Heavenly Father, I repent of my sins. I believe You sent Your Son Jesus to pay the penalty for those sins. I believe Jesus died and rose again; therefore, I ask You to come into my heart and be my Lord and Savior.*

*Congrats you're done.
You kept afloat!*

# **LIFE LESSONS**

Your life experiences are valuable. Being able to write allows you to grow, heal, and be free. Don't judge yourself. Don't edit; write to release your emotions. Grace has brought us this far.

> And he said unto me, My grace is sufficient for thee: for my strength is made perfect in weakness. Most gladly therefore will I rather glory in my infirmities, that the power of Christ may rest upon me. (2 Corinthians 12:9)

Do you believe that God's grace is sufficient for you? What challenges you not to believe?

_____

_____

_____

_____

_____

_____

_____

_____

_____

_____

_____

_____

# LIFE LESSONS

> But he giveth more grace. Wherefore he saith, God resisteth the proud, but giveth grace unto the humble.
> (James 4:6)

Why does God resist pride and give grace to the humble? What category do you honestly feel you are in? Do a self-check. Are you proud or humble? What adjustments can you make? Self-inventory is powerful.

LIFE LESSONS

> But by the grace of God I am what I am: and his grace which was bestowed upon me was not in vain, but I laboured more abundantly than they all: yet not I, but the grace of God which was with me.
>
> (1 Corinthians 15:10)

Explain why God's grace that is bestowed upon you is not in vain. Make your explanation personal.

_____
_____
_____
_____
_____
_____
_____
_____
_____
_____
_____
_____
_____
_____
_____
_____

# LIFE LESSONS

Breathe in and then breathe out. Are you ready? Write five positive attributes about yourself and pick one attribute you have fought hard to be strong in. Explain how you did it.

# LIFE LESSONS

Find an old picture of yourself and evaluate who you were in that picture and how you have grown. Challenge yourself to be honest. Grace brought you from a long way.

LIFE LESSONS

> Be sober, be vigilant; because your adversary the devil walks about like a roaring lion, seeking whom he may devour. (1 Peter 5:8, NKJV)

You have an enemy. His name is Satan. Explain a time in your life when you knew God's grace covered you? Add a scripture that supports your answer.

_____
_____
_____
_____
_____
_____
_____
_____
_____
_____
_____
_____
_____
_____
_____
_____

# LIFE LESSONS

> For I know the thoughts that I think toward you, says the Lord, thoughts of peace and not of evil, to give you a future and a hope. (Jeremiah 29:11, NKJV)

You are reminiscing on that one failure that has crippled you. God is your strength and song. Why do you rehearse the failure rather than moving forward?

___

___

___

___

___

___

___

___

___

___

___

___

___

___

___

___

___

___

# LIFE LESSONS

God shows both mercy and grace, but they are not the same. Often grace has been misunderstood. Explain your feelings of God's grace and His mercy.

# LIFE LESSONS

Grace is used to pardoning us when we have walked in error. How have you used grace as an excuse to be disobedient or to feel justified? Take the challenge and be honest with yourself.

_____
_____
_____
_____
_____
_____
_____
_____
_____
_____
_____
_____
_____
_____
_____
_____
_____
_____
_____
_____
_____
_____
_____

# LIFE LESSONS

You are the problem solver that your family, church, and community have been waiting for. What question would you ask God to grace you to solve and why?

# LIFE LESSONS

Write a 3 to 4-point strategy against the Enemy that would help someone to defeat him. Apply the following scripture to support your plan.

> Let us therefore come boldly to the throne of grace, that we may obtain mercy and find grace to help in time of need. (Hebrews 4:16, NKJV)

LIFE LESSONS

Please select a subject from this book and compare it to a situation in your life when grace was present. Write the parallel to help someone evolve.

LIFE LESSONS

Write a prayer of grace and send it to someone you know who needs encouragement. Speak life to the person declaring his/her victorious outcome.

# LIFE LESSONS

# OTHER BOOKS BY LADY KEMP

### Better than Yesterday: Proverbs of a Woman's Heart

We are often trapped in a prison of yesterday's sorrows, relentlessly taunted by our past, and dwelling on the saddest words "if only." If you desire to let go and move from a life of rejection to acceptance, want your todays to exceed your yesterdays, and journey to a brighter future, this series is for you.

The workbook presents a simple, yet, practical, interactive, self-reflective format. Used by groups or individuals, it can easily be adapted to suit the requirements for either. As you progress through the series, ponder its truths and complete the exercises, you will develop the tools to defeat the enemy of your past and reach a better tomorrow. Do the work to break free and stay free.

6" x 9" | 202 Full-Color Pages
9781562293550  Hardcover
9781562293604  Paperback
9781562298104  eBook

8.5" x 11" | 54 Pages
9781562293598  Workbook

Available wherever books are sold or from
ChristianLivingBooks.com

# ACKNOWLEDGMENTS

I'm so honored and delighted to complete this book. Here is a huge thanks to the amazing people who helped to make this assignment complete. To God be all the glory!

Christian Living Books, Inc.–you make all things lovely and special. Kimberly Stewart, you have become my sister and my publisher. Your expertise and unwavering dedication to *Better than Yesterday* and *Grace in Deep Waters* are amazing. You stretch me to do my best when I feel I have nothing else to write. You have inspired me to work harder at my creativity. Thank you, for being great in my life as a publisher. This is book two and three is next. Grace! This book collaboration is amazing in my eyes. I honor you!

Shelia Joseph–you are a gift, so unselfish. When I thought I was on my own with this second book, you said, "No, I'm with you." You are so generous and loyal in helping me to be the best at what I strive to do in writing. Your honesty and love are what I admire. Thank you, for sacrificing your time and efforts to ensure I completed this book. You are an amazing editor, and I am blessed to have you in my life. You could have said no not this time, but you believed in me. I pray you are with me in book three (lol). Your intelligence and the ability to multitask are gifts. Thank you; I love you!

Mr. Daniel and Mrs. Geneva Jordan of D Jordan Photographic, my family–you continue to take this journey with me, and I am very grateful. You go over and beyond to ensure all goes well with my photography. I am blessed to be your little sister. When I told you the vision for my pictures although I cannot swim (lol), you ensured we got it done, and I was safe. There were lots of laughs and adventures on picture day and what a beautiful outcome. My big sister, Geneva, thank you for your constant encouragement and for reminding me of the value of faith. Thank you! Love always.

Thank you to each endorser for your written endorsements in this book. We all come from different walks of life and have experienced God's grace on many levels. I have so much gratitude for you for saying yes and choosing to be a part of *Grace in Deep Waters*. I am confident your insightful words will inspire the readers to dig deep and look into their own lives when grace was present. I pray blessings upon blessings on your lives. I value your time and sacrifices. I thank you!

While evolving is beautiful, the journey to it is not a homerun. Some incredible people have made my journey easier and better. Thank you to my mentor Prophetess Bridgett Barnes for pouring into my life. Your master class and one on one time has helped to make me a better person. Thank you for the years of pouring into me constantly and without judgement. I love you sissy!

# SPECIAL THANKS

My family–I love you dearly. I feel so blessed that God gave me all of you. God blessed me with four brothers and three sisters-in-love: James, Robert and Ruscell, Daniel and Geneva, and Jerry and Vicky. Family is God's gift. Family is you. I'm thankful for being your little sister. To my nieces, nephews, and entire family, I love you all dearly. You don't get to pick your family; you love and cherish the family God gives you. I praise God I have you all.

Greater Harvest Christian Center–the love you show me is priceless. From the depths of my heart, I thank you for your prayers and amazing support. You are a great church, and I'm honored to have your encouragement. We are 20 years in ministry this year. God is faithful. Because of grace, we are taking new dimensions and territories. I love you church family. Christian Women of Faith and Fellowship, you have a special place in my heart. Thank you for your love, creativity, and faithful inspiration to me. I honor you!

To my village–we laugh until we cry. My sisterhood, you are my strength and song. I love you so much. Regina Shelton, Deanna Lewis, Mechelle Henry, Marika Walker, Tonya Bealey, Stacey Williams, and Shawn Myers Clark–40-plus years of friendship, our village is family. We are growing older together; we are in our 50s. Wow! God is good to us. We share, travel, and celebrate with one another. The love we have for each other is truly rare, and I value us. Our husbands are brothers; it does not get any better than that. I love them so much. We have many more memories to create. Thank you for always supporting and encouraging me. You can always count on me.

To my Auntie Pinkie Price (my mom's only living sister), I call you Auntie Shug–I love you and I'm grateful for you. You are one of the strongest women I know. I admire you. Janice, my sister, I've loved you all my life from the time I followed you around when I was a little girl. I thank God for you Sistah. Thank you for always encouraging and praying for me.

To Pamela Shakir and Raquel Elish Browden–I thank God for the years. You have been a support with this assignment from the beginning. I can call you at any hour of the day or night. I thank you for being you. We laugh and we cry. We talk about the Lord, and living well often. Thank you for the push to keep going and your daily prayers. You both have grown so much. I am so proud of you. Raquel your father would be so proud of you. I love you, little sisters!

Dr. Angel Schaffer, there is not one prayer request or doctor appointment that you forget. You keep each request in your bible and before the Lord. You remember before I do and remind me of each blessing. I thank you for being a prayer warrior to my family. You have had a great impact on my life, and I honor you for your being a woman that every sister needs to have.

God has blessed me to have incredible sister friends and First Ladies in my life. I want to thank each of you who have played a part in my becoming. Thank you for every experience. Thank you for every form of encouragement. Thank you for being there in the highs. Thank you for being there in the lows. All of it was necessary. My prayer for you is that God continues to give you grace in deep waters. Your genuine love for me has not gone unnoticed. I appreciate you all. Your support has been faithful and true. Without calling your names for there are too many, you know who you are. I am thankful for your special place in my heart. I love you dearly!

Because of God's grace! To God be all the glory!

# In Memory Of

Deborah Hawkins–our granny and wisdom, you will forever be in my heart. I honor you. I will never forget your encouragement, truths, and phone calls. You were always on time with the truth. Thank you to my sister, DeAnna Lewis, for bringing an amazing woman into my life. I will make her proud. You used *Better than Yesterday* as a teaching resource and encouraged me to keep writing. Your voice is yet loud in my heart. You were an extraordinary woman!

"Mama Mickey" Maria Sturdivant–you are forever in our hearts. We will model your zest for hard work and love for helping those less fortunate. I love you, Mama. Your smile and laughter are yet in my fondest memories of you. You were a giant in community service. Your love and unselfishness were contagious.

Our brother, Walker A. Williams, Jr.–grace carried our village when you left to be with the Father. Grace is ever-present to take us through. Your laugher and love will forever be cherished in our hearts. We promised to take great care of our dear sister Stacey and the girls, your angels. Promise. Your passion for life will forever be rooted in my heart. I'm grateful for the years of knowing and loving you.

## ABOUT THE AUTHOR

Lady Vicki Lynne Kemp was born to the proud parents of the late Pastor Daniel and Evangelist Cora Jordan. She has been married to her friend, Bishop Vernon R. Kemp, for 29 years. Lady Kemp has served with her husband at Greater Harvest Christian Center for 20 years. God has blessed this union with gifted and anointed children.

Lady Kemp serves as the Women's Ministry Administrator; she has a passion for encouraging women to be stronger emotionally, mentally, and spiritually. She also provides leadership on the Board of Scholastic Education of Greater Harvest Christian Center where she devotes her time to developing educational strategies to help students win. She also serves Kern High School as a youth empowerment speaker for Young Women Empowered for Leadership. She formerly served on the Board of Directors of Bakersfield Senior Center of Kern County.

Lady Kemp received her Evangelist License in December 2004. God has graced her to travel and minister the gospel of Jesus Christ. On August 1, 2018, Lady Kemp retired after 17 years as a full-time employee for Kern Regional Center in Bakersfield, CA where she served as a social worker for the special needs population of Kern County. Lady Kemp earned her bachelor's degree in liberal studies from California State University Bakersfield in 1996.

Along with her spiritual accomplishments, Lady Kemp is the author of *Better than Yesterday: Proverbs of a Woman's Heart.* Her book was selected for inclusion in the permanent collection by the Library of Congress on November 21, 2018, which is one of the highest honors an author can achieve. Christian Living Books, Inc. also awarded her the distinction, Best-Selling Author.

Adding to her entrepreneurship, Lady Kemp and her husband are investment partners with Fatburger Bakersfield. You can connect with Lady Kemp and join the conversation on her Saving Our Sisters podcast listed as VickiLKemp's Podcast, heard on Deezer, Iheartradio, Apple Podcast, Google Play, and Spotify. Through these podcasts and her weekly prayer on Facebook live entitled "Early Will I Seek Thee," she empowers women to evolve and become better.

Lady Kemp is the founder of Harvest of Hope Educational Services, which was birthed on August 9, 2016. This educational component is a branch of Greater Harvest Christian Center. She has a kingdom agenda to reach lost souls for Christ while also challenging and empowering youth to be successful in education. Her unwavering faith, compassion, selflessness, and incessant prayers speak volumes about her character and epitomize an undeniable and genuine love for God and His people. Lady Kemp's favorite statement is, "There is absolutely nothing too hard for our great God."

## Connect with Lady Kemp

- @LadyVKemp
- LadyVickiLKemp
- Vicki Kemp
- KempVicki@aol.com

- Author Page – Vicki Kemp - Author
- VickiLynneKemp.com
- Business Email – UAreBetterThanYesterday@gmail.com

# ENDNOTES

i. https://www.goodreads.com/quotes/tag/grace?page=2
ii. https://www.scq.ubc.ca/waiting-to-inhale-why-it-hurts-to-hold-your-breath/
iii. Kemp, Vicki L. (2018). *Better than Yesterday: Proverbs of a Woman's Heart.* Largo, MD: Christian Living Books.
iv. Crocker, M., & Houston, J. (2014). Oceans (Where Feet May Fail) [Recorded by 1276407283 942153028 S. Lightelm]. On *Zion* [CD]. Sydney, Australia: Hillsong Church T/A Hillsong Music Australia. (2013, August 23)
v. http://anointedmessagesnotes.blogspot.com/2014/09/finishing-grace-joel-osteen.html
vi. https://www.poetrysoup.com/poem/swimming_against_the_tide_1019690
vii. http://thinkexist.com/quotation/the_winds_of_grace_are_always_blowing-all_we_need/14248.html
viii. http://thinkexist.com/quotation/happiness_cannot_be_traveled_to-owned-earned-worn/296673.html
ix. https://www.thegospelcoalition.org/article/grace-sufficient-for-today/
x. https://www.desiringgod.org/interviews/what-is-gods-glory--2
xi. https://renner.org/devil-has-a-plan-for-your-life/
xii. https://www.thegospelcoalition.org/article/god-can-restor-your-lost-years/

www.ingramcontent.com/pod-product-compliance
Lightning Source LLC
Chambersburg PA
CBHW040251170426
43191CB00018B/2369